GOVERNMENT PROCEDURES AND OPERATIONS

MODERNIZATION OF THE GOVERNMENT PERFORMANCE AND RESULTS ACT (GPRA)

GOVERNMENT PROCEDURES AND OPERATIONS

Additional books in this series can be found on Nova's website under the Series tab.

Additional E-books in this series can be found on Nova's website under the E-book tab.

AMERICAN POLITICAL, ECONOMIC AND SECURITY ISSUES

Additional books in this series can be found on Nova's website under the Series tab.

Additional E-books in this series can be found on Nova's website under the E-book tab.

GOVERNMENT PROCEDURES AND OPERATIONS

MODERNIZATION OF THE GOVERNMENT PERFORMANCE AND RESULTS ACT (GPRA)

RAY HAWKINS

AND

TRAVIS P. DUNCAN

EDITORS

NOVINKA

New York

For permission to use material from this book please contact us:
Telephone 631-231-7269; Fax 631-231-8175
Web Site: http://www.novapublishers.com

LIBRARY OF CONGRESS CATALOGING-IN-PUBLICATION DATA

ISBN: 978-1-62257-383-7

Published by Nova Science Publishers, Inc. † New York

CONTENTS

PREFACE

On January 4th, 2011, the GPRA Modernization Act of 2010 became law. The acronym refers to the Government Performance and Results Act. When GPRA 1993 was enacted, it was regarded as a watershed for the federal government. For the first time, Congress established requirements in statute for most agencies to set goals, measure performance, and report the information to Congress for potential use. Agencies submitted this information in three major products: multi-year strategic plans, annual plans, and annual reports. This book provides an overview and background on GPRA 1993 and its modernization changes in 2010. The law was especially intended to address the needs of Congress in its policy making, oversight, and budgeting work, and the needs of agency program managers.

Chapter 1 - On January 4, 2011, the GPRA Modernization Act of 2010 (GPRAMA) became law. The acronym "GPRA" in the act's short title refers to the Government Performance and Results Act of 1993 (GPRA 1993), a law that GPRAMA substantially modified. When GPRA 1993 was enacted, it was regarded as a watershed for the federal government. For the first time, Congress established statutory requirements for most agencies to set goals, measure performance, and submit related plans and reports (hereafter, "products") to Congress for its potential use.

Chapter 2 - The federal government is the world's largest and most complex entity, with about $3.5 trillion in outlays in fiscal year 2010 that fund a broad array of programs and operations. GAO's long-term simulations of the federal budget show—absent policy change—growing deficits accumulating to an unsustainable increase in debt. While the spending side is driven by rising health care costs and demographics, other areas should also be scrutinized. In addition, there are significant performance and management challenges that the federal government needs to confront.

GAO was asked to testify on the Government Performance and Results Act (GPRA) Modernization Act of 2010 (GPRAMA), as the administration begins implementing the act. This statement is based on GAO's past and ongoing work on GPRA implementation, as well as recently issued reports (1) identifying opportunities to reduce potential duplication in government programs, save tax dollars, and enhance revenue; and (2) updating GAO's list of government operations at high risk due to their greater vulnerabilities to fraud, waste, abuse, and mismanagement, or the need for transformation. As required by GPRAMA, GAO will periodically evaluate implementation of the act and report to Congress on its findings and recommendations.

Chapter 3 - The Committee on Homeland Security and Governmental Affairs, to which was referred the bill (H.R. 2142) to require quarterly performance assessments of Government programs for purposes of assessing agency performance and improvement, and to establish agency performance improvement officers and the Performance Improvement Council, having considered the same, reports favorably thereon with an amendment in the nature of a substitute, and recommends that the bill, as amended, do pass.

In: Modernization of the Government ... ISBN: 978-1-62257-383-7
Editors: R. Hawkins and T. P. Duncan

Chapter 1

CHANGES TO THE GOVERNMENT PERFORMANCE AND RESULTS ACT (GPRA): OVERVIEW OF THE NEW FRAMEWORK OF PRODUCTS AND PROCESSES*

Clinton T. Brass

SUMMARY

On January 4, 2011, the GPRA Modernization Act of 2010 (GPRAMA) became law. The acronym "GPRA" in the act's short title refers to the Government Performance and Results Act of 1993 (GPRA 1993), a law that GPRAMA substantially modified. When GPRA 1993 was enacted, it was regarded as a watershed for the federal government. For the first time, Congress established statutory requirements for most agencies to set goals, measure performance, and submit related plans and reports (hereafter, "products") to Congress for its potential use.

After a four-year phase-in period for GPRA 1993 and 13 years of the law's full implementation, GPRAMA makes substantial changes. Among other things, GPRAMA

* This is an edited, reformatted and augmented version of the Congressional Research Service Publication R42379, dated February 29, 2012.

- continues three agency-level products from GPRA 1993, but with changes;
- establishes new products and processes that focus on goal-setting and performance measurement in policy areas that cut across agencies;
- brings attention to using goals and measures during policy implementation;
- increases reporting on the Internet; and
- requires individuals to be responsible for some goals and management tasks.

In making these changes, GPRAMA aligns the timing of many products to coincide with presidential terms and budget proposals. The law also includes more central roles for the Office of Management and Budget (OMB), an entity that often seeks to advance the President's policy preferences. GPRAMA also contains more specific requirements for consultations with Congress.

By design, many of GPRAMA's products are required to be submitted to Congress for scrutiny and potential use. The law also provides opportunities for Congress and non-federal stakeholders to influence how agencies and OMB set goals and assess performance. This report provides an overview of GPRAMA's products and processes. In addition, the report highlights potential issues for Congress. Related questions that Congress might consider include the following:

- Are agencies' and OMB's consultations with Congress working well? Are agencies and OMB defining goals and assessing performance in ways that reflect underlying statutes and congressional intent?
- Are the representations that agencies and OMB make about government performance perceived by Congress, federal personnel, and the public as credible and useful? What are the implications of evidence that is presented?
- Are agencies and OMB implementing GPRAMA with desired levels of transparency and public participation?
- Are agencies, OMB, and Congress focusing effectively on crosscutting policy areas to better coordinate efforts and reduce any unnecessary duplication?
- Are agencies and OMB implementing GPRAMA in a responsive, effective manner? Is GPRAMA working well? If not, what might be done?

On January 4, 2011, the GPRA Modernization Act of 2010 (GPRAMA) became law.[1] The acronym "GPRA" in the act's short title refers to the Government Performance and Results Act of 1993 (GPRA 1993), a law that GPRAMA substantially modified.[2] When GPRA 1993 was enacted, it was regarded as a watershed for the federal government. For the first time, Congress established requirements in statute for most agencies to set goals, measure performance, and report the information to Congress for potential use.[3] Agencies submitted this information in three major products: multi-year strategic plans, annual plans, and annual reports. The law also required agencies to consult with Congress and non-federal stakeholders when developing some of these plans and goals. As a thread running through these requirements, the authors of GPRA 1993 said the law especially was intended to address the needs of Congress in its policy making, oversight, and budgeting work, and the needs of agency program managers.[4]

After a four-year phase-in period for GPRA 1993 and 13 years of the law's full implementation, GPRAMA makes substantial changes. Among other things, GPRAMA

- continues the three agency-level products from GPRA 1993, but with changes;
- establishes new products and processes that focus on goal-setting and performance measurement in policy areas that cut across agencies;
- brings attention to using goals and measures during policy implementation;
- increases reporting on the Internet; and
- requires individuals to be responsible for some goals and management tasks.

In making these changes, GPRAMA aligns the timing of many products to coincide with presidential terms and budget proposals.[5] The law also includes more central roles for the Office of Management and Budget (OMB), an entity that often seeks to advance the President's policy preferences. GPRAMA also contains more specific requirements for consultations with Congress.

By design, many of GPRAMA's products are required to be submitted to Congress for scrutiny and potential use. The law also provides opportunities for Congress and non-federal stakeholders to influence how agencies and OMB set goals and assess performance. This report provides an overview of GPRAMA's products and processes. In addition, the report highlights potential issues for Congress. To provide context, the report first identifies potential congressional roles that relate to performance. Furthermore, because GPRAMA inserts an extensive vocabulary into law and practice, the report also includes a list of acronyms (Appendix A) and glossary (Appendix B).

BACKGROUND: CONGRESS AND PERFORMANCE

The roles that Congress may take regarding government performance are pervasive and difficult to overstate. In exercising its constitutional powers, Congress may by law establish agencies, their missions and goals, processes for how they operate, their priorities, and their resource levels. Congress also may influence the actions of agencies and OMB through non-statutory means, conduct oversight, and study policy problems. In any of these activities, Congress may cooperate or compete with the President to influence how agencies implement public policies.

ILLUSTRATIONS OF PROGRAM EVALUATION AND PERFORMANCE MEASUREMENT

A federal program might focus on helping homeless veterans and reducing their rate of homelessness. In this context, a program evaluation might address the question whether the program is reducing the rate of homelessness in comparison to what would have happened in the absence of the federal program. A program evaluation also might assess whether the program's services are meeting the needs of clients. Performance measurement, by contrast, focuses on counting things such as the number of services provided or the overall homelessness rate. Typically, both program evaluation and performance measurement are helpful sources of information. They answer different kinds of questions, however.

Like GPRA 1993, GPRAMA provides for goal-setting, measurement, and evaluation. These activities may not always be pursued in a neutral way, however. The choice of a policy goal or a trade-off among goals may be contested. It could be argued, therefore, that goals are inherently political in nature. Similarly, the definition of "success" that is to be used when assessing a program's performance also may be contested. In these situations, two tools of policy analysis often are used to help inform assessments of performance: program evaluation and performance measurement. Program evaluations use one or more methods to assess how, and the extent to which, programs or policies achieve intended objectives or cause unintended consequences (see box at right). By contrast, performance measurement is narrower in scope. It refers to periodic measurement of data that are related to programs. Used in isolation, performance measures do not necessarily reflect how well a program is working, because measurements may be driven by so-called "external factors" that are separate from the program, such as a natural disaster or downturn in the economy. In response, measurement and evaluation may be used together to help inform policy making. Policy making also may be informed by a variety of other analyses and considerations, such as forecasting, logic, risk assessment, and values.

In this context, Congress may assume at least two roles. First, when Congress looks at a specific program or policy area, Congress may use performance information to help inform its thinking, oversight, and policy making. For example, an interest group or the President may cite goals, evaluations, and measures when justifying a proposal to Congress. Congress and other consumers of performance information may face challenges in these situations—such as when scrutinizing whether information has been presented without bias or is relevant to a policy problem. A large volume of incoming information also may strain time and staff resources. Challenges like these highlight another potential role. In this second role, Congress may establish federal policies and processes that relate to how the government's goal-setting, planning, and evaluation are to be conducted.

Congress's passage of GPRA 1993 and GPRAMA are examples of this role. In addition, Congress may require agencies to involve non-federal stakeholders in processes like goal-setting or direct agencies to act transparently. In these ways, stakeholders may help Congress to identify performance-related issues that merit closer attention.[6]

Policies and processes like these typically are intended to generate useful information for multiple audiences—including Congress, agencies, the President, and the public—and, thereby, to help inform policy making, oversight, and faithful and effective implementation of laws.

This chapter focuses primarily on the first role, regarding the information and opportunities that GPRAMA may generate.[7] Nevertheless, Congress might also assume the second role if it were assessing GPRAMA's design and implementation or considering changes to the law.

GPRAMA's Products and Processes

GPRAMA substantially modified and added to GPRA 1993's framework of products and processes. In making these changes, GPRAMA's design drew from multiple sources. These included the views of the law's authors, the Barack Obama Administration's approach to government performance, the George W. Bush Administration's approach to government performance, the work during the 111th Congress of a Senate Budget Committee task force, and Government Accountability Office (GAO) views.[8] Looking ahead, these influences and the federal government's experience with GPRA 1993 may provide insights into current issues of GPRAMA's design, implementation, and prospects. This report, however, focuses more immediately on GPRAMA's statutory requirements and the information and opportunities that the law may generate for Congress. In that light, the following subsections discuss GPRAMA's major provisions in four categories:

- agency-level products and processes that GPRAMA continues from GPRA 1993, albeit with significant changes;[9]
- new agency-level products and processes;
- new products and processes that are executive branch-wide in scope; and
- institutional changes.[10]

After reviewing these provisions, subsequent sections of this chapter discuss how the changes fit together, some of their potential implications, and potential issues for Congress.

Agency-Level Products and Processes Continuing from GPRA 1993

GPRAMA retains the three agency-level products that GPRA 1993 created. However, the law provides the products with new statutory names, inserts additional requirements, and makes several changes to their schedules and processes for being developed.[11]

- **Agency Strategic Plan (ASP; formerly Strategic Plan).** GPRAMA requires an agency to post a four-year Agency Strategic Plan on its public website.[12]
  - *Contents.* Some provisions from GPRA 1993 remain unchanged. Like GPRA 1993, GPRAMA requires an Agency Strategic Plan to identify "general goals and objectives" for the major functions and operations of the agency and to describe the evaluations used in establishing goals and objectives. GPRAMA also adds new requirements. Among other things, an agency must describe how it is working with other agencies to achieve certain goals.
  - *Timing requirements.* GPRAMA newly aligns the process of developing and updating an Agency Strategic Plan to coincide with presidential terms and budget proposals. An ASP must cover four fiscal years and must be updated every four years. An agency is required to submit the revised plan just after the first year of a President's term, by the first Monday in February—the same deadline as the President's annual budget proposal.[13] In the transition from GPRA 1993, GPRAMA requires agencies to adjust the Strategic Plans that they developed under GPRA 1993 to conform to GPRAMA's requirements by the deadline for the President's FY2013 budget proposal, in February 2012. Thereafter, agencies are required to submit revised ASPs just after the first year of each presidential term (e.g., February 2014).
  - *Agency consultations with Congress and non-federal stakeholders.* Like GPRA 1993, GPRAMA requires agencies to involve Congress and stakeholders in the development of Agency Strategic Plans. However, GPRAMA provides more specific requirements for how agencies are required to consult with Congress. When developing or adjusting an ASP, an agency is required to consult "periodically" with Congress, including majority and minority views from the "appropriate" authorizing, appropriations, and oversight committees. Agencies also are required to consult with "appropriate" committees of Congress every two years, regardless of whether an ASP is updated.[14] When developing or adjusting an ASP, an agency also is required to solicit and consider the views and suggestions of stakeholders.[15]

- **Agency Performance Plan (APP; formerly Annual Performance Plan)**. GPRAMA requires an agency annually to post an Agency Performance Plan on its public website. The plan accompanies the agency's budget proposal, as submitted by the President or the agency.[16] The APP is required to cover each "program activity" (portion of a budget account; see Appendix B), as presented in the *Appendix* volume of the President's budget proposal to Congress.
  - *Contents*. Like GPRA 1993, GPRAMA requires an Agency Performance Plan to establish one or more "performance goals."[17] An APP is required to establish performance indicators to be used in measuring or assessing progress toward these performance goals. Indicators may be of many types, including efficiency, outputs, and outcomes.[18] Under GPRAMA, the APP has new requirements, as well. For example, the product must describe how an agency plans to address major management challenges. In addition, the APP must identify "low-priority program activities" and provide an "evidence-based justification" for the low-priority designation. The product also is required to identify agency officials, called "goal leaders," who are responsible for the achievement of each performance goal.
  - *Time coverage*. GPRAMA continues the GPRA 1993 requirement for the Agency Performance Plan to cover the forthcoming fiscal year, to coincide with the agency's budget request. Newly, however, the law also requires the APP to cover the current year in which the plan is submitted. Consequently, the APP becomes a two-year goal-setting product, in which the plan covers the forthcoming year and also updates goals and other information for the current year that were included in the previous year's APP.[19]
- **Agency Performance Update (APU; formerly Program Performance Report)**. GPRAMA requires that an "update on agency performance" be made available each year on the agency's public website.[20]
  - *Contents*. Continuing from GPRA 1993, GPRAMA requires the Agency Performance Update to provide performance indicators from the relevant Agency Performance Plan and compare performance goals with actual results. If a past performance goal was not met, an agency's APU is required to explain why and to describe plans for achieving the goal or explain if the goal is infeasible. Under GPRAMA, the APU also is newly required to

provide data of significant value more frequently than annually if this can be done at a "reasonable" level of administrative burden.

- *Timing requirements.* The authors of GPRAMA probably intended for the Agency Performance Update to be made available no later than 150 days after the end of the fiscal year.[21] In practice, agencies probably will comply with the APU's requirements sooner than the 150-day deadline. Depending on how an agency wishes to comply with current law and OMB direction, the APU may be completed (1) in November, several weeks after the end of a fiscal year, or (2) in February of the next calendar year, accompanying the agency's budget request and Agency Performance Plan.[22]

New Agency-Level Products and Processes

At the agency level, GPRAMA adds new requirements for goal-setting, implementation reviews, and plans and reports.

- **Agency priority goals (APGs)**. Every two years, GPRAMA requires the heads of certain executive agencies—the so-called CFO Act agencies plus any additional agencies designated by OMB—to identify a small subset of the performance goals from their Agency Performance Plans.[23] These goals are to be identified as "agency priority goals" (APGs). Agencies are required to identify an agency official, called a goal leader, who is responsible for achieving each APG.
    - *Process, timing, and role of OMB.* GPRAMA requires agency priority goals to be identified beginning with each agency's FY2013 Agency Performance Plan. Apart from this requirement, GPRAMA establishes a potentially central role for OMB in structuring the APG process. The law provides that OMB determines the total number of agency priority goals and the number of goals to be developed by each agency. The law also appears to allow OMB to choose APGs and to determine the schedule for identifying them.[24]
    - *Determining priorities.* GPRAMA requires these goals to "reflect the highest priorities of the agency," as determined by the head of the agency and informed by two sources: OMB-developed

"federal government priority goals" (see next section, under "New Executive Branch-Wide Products and Processes") and an agency's consultations regarding its Agency Strategic Plan. However, the law does not require agencies or OMB to consult with Congress or stakeholders when they identify agency priority goals.

- **Quarterly reviews for agency priority goals**. During each fiscal year, GPRAMA requires an agency head and deputy head to conduct a "quarterly priority progress review." The quarterly review is required to focus on progress toward achieving each agency priority goal. GPRAMA's provisions appear to be modeled on the Obama Administration's "high-priority performance goal" (HPPG) initiative, where reviews were conducted as in-person meetings.[25]
  - *Timing requirements*. The reviews were required to begin for the third quarter of FY2011 based on HPPGs from the President's FY2011 budget proposal. After agencies made available their FY2013 Agency Performance Plans, GPRAMA required the reviews to be based on agency priority goals.
  - *Transparency*. GPRAMA does not require the reviews themselves to be transparent to Congress or the public. Some information about APGs is required to be included on an OMB-developed website (see next section, under "New Executive Branch-Wide Products and Processes").
- **"Unmet goal" reports and plans**. GPRAMA requires OMB to annually determine whether an agency meets the performance goals in its Agency Performance Plan, or whether any goals are "unmet." Using these determinations, agencies and OMB are required to generate several kinds of reports and plans to address unmet goals.[26] Under GPRAMA, agency priority goals are subject to these requirements, because they are performance goals that are required to be included in an agency's APP.
- **Lists of plans and reports produced for Congress**. GPRAMA requires an agency to annually list all plans and reports it produces for Congress that are required by statute or directed in congressional reports. From this list, the agency is required to identify a minimum percentage of the products as "outdated" or "duplicative." GPRAMA provides that the minimum percentage is to be determined annually by OMB but must be at least 10% in the first year of GPRAMA's implementation. The agency is required to submit this second list to

OMB. Next, GPRAMA requires the agency to consult with congressional committees that receive the documents to determine whether the products are no longer useful to them and could be eliminated or consolidated.

New Executive Branch-Wide Products and Processes

At the executive branch-wide level, GPRAMA adds new requirements for goal-setting, plans, implementation reviews, and reports.

- **Federal government priority goals (FGPGs)**. OMB is required to work with agencies to develop long-term "federal government priority goals" (FGPGs).
  - *Contents*. Federal government priority goals are required to be developed in two categories: (1) outcome-oriented goals in a limited number of policy areas that cut across agency boundaries, and (2) goals for management improvements across the federal government. In the second category, goals may relate to improvements in financial management, human capital management, information technology management, procurement and acquisition management, and real property management.
  - *Timing requirements*. GPRAMA aligns the process of developing federal government priority goals to coincide with the deadline for submitting the President's budget proposal just after the first year of his or her term. The goals are required to be updated or revised every four years according to this schedule. In the transition from GPRA 1993, GPRAMA requires interim FGPGs to be submitted with the President's FY2013 budget proposal.
  - *OMB consultations with Congress*. When OMB develops or adjusts FGPGs, GPRAMA requires OMB to consult "periodically" with the majorities and minorities of several specific committees (see Appendix B) and any other "appropriate" committees. OMB also is required to consult at least once every two years with "appropriate committees," presumably about FGPGs.
- **Federal Government Performance Plan (FGPP)**. GPRAMA requires OMB to coordinate with agencies to develop an annual Federal Government Performance Plan (FGPP).[27] OMB is required to

submit the plan to Congress with the President's budget proposals for FY2013 and each subsequent year.

- *Contents.* Among other things, the Federal Government Performance Plan is required to establish one or more "federal government performance goals" for each federal government priority goal. The plan also is required to identify a "lead Government official" to be responsible for coordinating efforts to achieve each federal government priority goal.
- *Time coverage.* Like the Agency Performance Plan, the FGPP is a two-year plan that covers the forthcoming year and the year in which the plan is submitted.

- **Quarterly reviews for FGPGs**. During each fiscal year, GPRAMA requires OMB to conduct a "quarterly priority progress review" of the progress toward achieving each federal government priority goal.
  - *Timing requirements.* The quarterly reviews are required to begin for the quarter ending June 30, 2012 (i.e., third quarter of FY2012).
  - *Transparency.* The law does not require the reviews themselves to be transparent to Congress or the public. Some information about federal government priority goals is required to be included on an OMB-developed website (see next bullet, below).
- **OMB performance website**. GPRAMA requires OMB to establish a single, performance-related website by October 1, 2012.[28] The website is required to be accessible to Congress and the public in a searchable, machine-readable format. With respect to content, GPRAMA requires the website to make available
  - information about the two kinds of "priority" goals that GPRAMA establishes—agency priority goals and federal government priority goals— including how both kinds of priority goals incorporate views and suggestions obtained through congressional consultations;
  - all information required for the Federal Government Performance Plan, posted concurrently with submission of the President's budget proposal;
  - agency-level Agency Strategic Plans, Agency Performance Plans, and Agency Performance Updates; and
  - detailed information about each "program" identified by agencies, including in each case an explanation of how the agency defines the term "program."[29]

GPRAMA requires the OMB performance website to be updated quarterly. It remains to be seen, however, which categories of data on the website will be updated on that schedule.[30] GPRAMA does not require the website to provide transparency into the quarterly reviews that OMB and agencies conduct for the two kinds of priority goals. Therefore, information from the reviews may or may not be posted online.

- **Presidential list of plans and reports for Congress**. GPRAMA requires the President's budget proposal to include an executive branch-wide list of certain plans and reports that agencies produce for Congress.
    - *Contents*. The President's list is required to include products "that agencies identified for elimination or consolidation because the plans and reports are determined outdated or duplicative of other required plans and reports."[31] GPRAMA further says OMB may concurrently submit draft legislation to eliminate or consolidate these products.
    - *Process*. As noted earlier, each agency is separately required to identify an OMB-determined percentage of reports and plans as outdated or duplicative, send this list to OMB, and consult with congressional recipients about which products could be eliminated or consolidated.[32] The agency-level requirement does not specify that agencies go beyond identifying reports and plans as outdated or duplicative to also identify them for elimination or consolidation. If agencies operate according to the sequence in the separate requirement, the President's list may not reflect agencies' consultations about whether any of the products are considered by recipients to be outdated or duplicative.

Institutional Changes

GPRAMA's provisions that relate to products and processes are accompanied by several institutional changes that involve officials and organizations. GPRAMA provides that the officials and organizations have specific duties in relation to many of the products and processes.

- **Chief Operating Officers (COOs)**. GPRAMA establishes an additional title for the deputy head or equivalent position of each agency: Chief Operating Officer (COO). GPRAMA says the agency's COO is "responsible for improving the management and performance of the agency" and specifies several corresponding functions. These include responsibility for assisting the agency head in implementing GPRAMA, conducting quarterly reviews for agency priority goals, and overseeing efforts to improve mission-support functions (e.g., procurement).

- **Performance Improvement Officers (PIOs)**. GPRAMA requires each agency head to designate a senior executive as Performance Improvement Officer (PIO).
    - *Qualification requirements and reporting relationship.* An agency's Performance Improvement Officer may be a career civil servant or a political appointee. GPRAMA does not identify specific qualification requirements. A PIO is required to report directly to the agency Chief Operating Officer.
    - *Duties.* The primary duties of a Performance Improvement Officer under GPRAMA are to advise and assist the head and deputy head of an agency in areas like goal-setting, planning, and performance measurement. A PIO also is required to assist with quarterly reviews of progress toward APGs and the "development and use ... of performance measures in personnel performance appraisals." GPRAMA does not explicitly provide for transparency outside the executive branch into the activities and agendas of individual PIOs.[33]
- **Performance Improvement Council (PIC)**. GPRAMA establishes in law a Performance Improvement Council (PIC).
    - *Membership.* The Performance Improvement Council's membership includes OMB's Deputy Director for Management (DDM) as chairperson, Performance Improvement Officers from the 24 CFO Act agencies, and other PIOs and individuals as determined by OMB's DDM.
    - *Duties.* The Performance Improvement Council's primary duties include assisting OMB with topics related to GPRAMA and serving at the direction of OMB's Deputy Director for Management, who determines the council's agenda and directs its work. The PIC also is tasked with developing related recommendations for the Director of OMB or the President, as specified by the DDM, and working to resolve crosscutting performance issues. GPRAMA does not explicitly provide for

transparency outside the executive branch into the PIC's activities and agenda.[34]

- **OMB-directed staff of agency personnel for the Performance Improvement Council**. GPRAMA requires each of the 24 CFO Act agencies, plus any other agencies with Performance Improvement Officers who serve as members of the Performance Improvement Council, to provide up to two "personnel authorizations" to serve at the direction of OMB's Deputy Director for Management upon his or her request.[35] If the reference to "personnel authorizations" were interpreted as requiring an agency to provide detailees, OMB could use this authority to direct 48 or more agency staff in support of the PIC's duties and the President's performance-related agenda.
- **Officials responsible for certain goals and topics**. As noted earlier, GPRAMA requires individual officials to be identified as responsible for certain topics. A consolidated listing of these topics and officials follows:
    - *Agency-level performance goals*. An Agency Performance Plan is required to identify the agency officials, called goal leaders, who are responsible for the achievement of each performance goal.
    - *Agency priority goals*. Agencies and the OMB performance website are required to identify an agency official, also called a goal leader, who is responsible for achieving each agency priority goal.
    - *Federal government priority goals*. The Federal Government Performance Plan and the OMB performance website are required to identify a lead government official to be responsible for coordinating efforts to achieve each federal government priority goal.
    - *Resolution of major management challenges*. An Agency Performance Plan is required to identify the agency official who is responsible for resolving major management challenges that the agency faces.
    - *Improvement strategies for unmet goals*. When OMB determines that an agency has not met one or more performance goals from its Agency Performance Plan for one year, the agency is required to designate a "senior official" to oversee "performance improvement strategies" for each goal.

VIEWING THE PRODUCTS AND PROCESSES TOGETHER

Implementation Schedule: Requirements and Deadlines

GPRAMA provides for many products and processes that will be presented to Congress. Each may be viewed in isolation. Several patterns emerge, however, when they are viewed together. Figure 1 provides a timeline for GPRAMA's implementation.

On the left side, the figure lists some of GPRAMA's requirements for products and processes. Items that are associated with GPRAMA appear as rectangles with light grey background and black print. For reference, the figure also includes the statutory requirement for the President's budget proposal (black background, white print), because GPRAMA aligns the schedules of several products to coincide with the President's budget proposal. At the bottom, timelines show fiscal and calendar years.

Moving from left to right, when the figure shows a vertical line that intersects with a product or process, GPRAMA requires the product or process to be submitted or initiated by that time.

Figure 1 illustrates several of GPRAMA's changes from prior practice and some patterns from GPRAMA's requirements. As noted earlier, three products associated with GPRA 1993 have new names, modified contents, and different years of coverage. For example, Agency Performance Plans are required to cover two fiscal years instead of only one.[36] The figure shows these revised requirements for successive APPs.

The figure also shows how Agency Strategic Plans are required to be adjusted with the FY2013 President's budget proposal and then submitted on a regular, four-year schedule beginning with the FY2015 President's budget proposal.

Separately, GPRAMA required agencies to commence with quarterly reviews of previously established high-priority performance goals based on performance during the third quarter of FY2011. GPRAMA requires agency priority goals to be included in FY2013 Agency Performance Plans and subject to quarterly reviews thereafter.

Subsequently, the schedule for establishing and revising agency priority goals may be determined by OMB. Consequently, the schedule for release of new or revised APGs may vary over time and differ among Presidents.

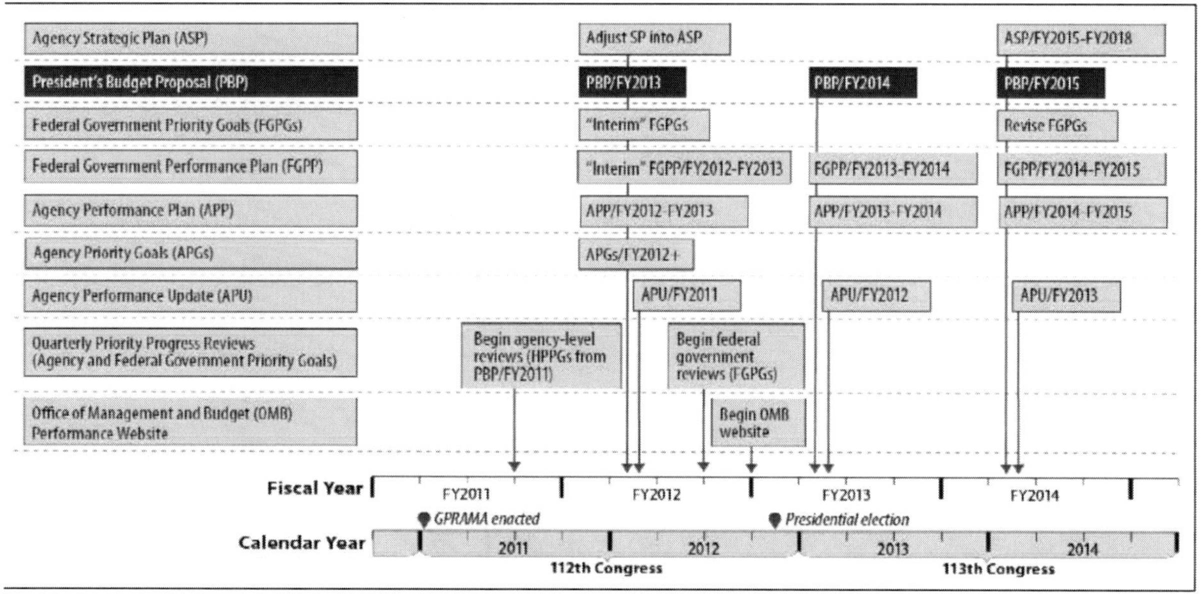

Source: CRS.

Notes: On the left side, GPRAMA's requirements for several products and processes are listed (gray background, black print). The figure also includes the statutory requirement for the President's budget proposal, for reference (black background, white print). When the figure shows a vertical line that intersects with a product or process, GPRAMA requires the product or process to be submitted or initiated by that time. For example, "PBP/FY2013" stands for the FY2013 President's budget proposal due by February 2012; and on the right side at the top, "ASP/FY2015-FY2018" stands for an Agency Strategic Plan that is due by February 2014 to cover the period FY2015-FY2018.

Figure 1. Timeline for GPRAMA Implementation: Requirements and Deadlines.

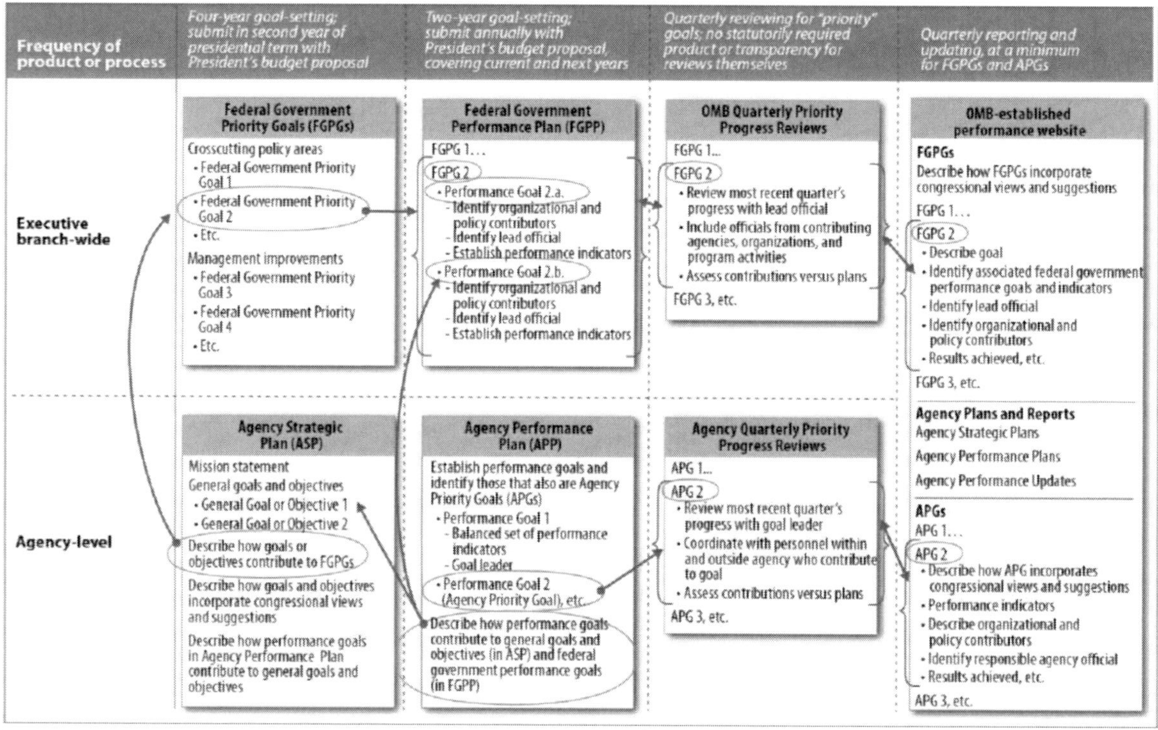

Source: CRS.

Notes: Arrows indicate relationships between the circled or bracketed information in different products and processes.

Figure 2. Illustrative Relationships among the Contents of Products and Processes.

With respect to deadlines, GPRAMA aligns the timing for many of its products with submission of the President's budget proposal, as shown by the vertical lines. Initially, the law requires the President, OMB, and agencies to produce several products to accompany the President's FY2013 budget proposal. However, GPRAMA provides that a one-year transition from GPRA 1993 take place. Consequently, the law characterizes some of these goals and plans as "interim" or "adjusted." After the FY2013 transition, full implementation begins with the President's budget proposals for FY2014 and FY2015. The FY2015 submission will occur just after the first year of the presidential term that begins in January 2013. The products that are due in February 2014 also illustrate how GPRAMA aligns Agency Strategic Plans and federal government priority goals with presidential terms.

Relationships among Contents of Products and Processes

By design, many of GPRAMA's products are required to be submitted to Congress as potential inputs for its work. The law directs, for example, that an Agency Performance Plan shall provide detailed information to Congress about the agency's goals, operations, and results. In considering the representations that these products make, Congress may examine each product in isolation. However, additional perspective may be gained by viewing how the contents of the products and processes relate each other. Figure 2 illustrates some of these interrelationships. In the figure, several products and processes are illustrated by graphics that contain small subsets of GPRAMA's detailed requirements. Agency-level products and processes are shown in the bottom row, and executive branch-wide products and processes are shown in the top row. Notably, while GPRA 1993 focused on agency-level products and processes, GPRAMA added several items at the executive branch-wide level. Moving from left to right across columns, Figure 2 shows how GPRAMA's products and processes reflect four-year goal-setting at both the executive branch-wide level and the agency level (second column), annual submission of two-year goal-setting (third column), quarterly reviews of priority goals (fourth column), and inclusion of information on the OMB website (fifth column). The OMB website is required to provide both agency-level and executive branch-wide information.

The figure illustrates how GPRAMA requires some of the contents of products and processes to relate to each other. For example, GPRAMA requires OMB to establish federal government priority goals. Inside the small graphic for FGPGs (upper left), Figure 2 circles a hypothetical federal government priority goal for a crosscutting policy area, labeled as "FGPG 2." This might be a goal related to food safety, for example, where multiple agencies and programs work to promote a safe national food supply. The figure then uses arrows to trace how other products and processes at the executive branch-wide and agency levels are required to relate to that goal. Moving to the right, the Federal Government Performance Plan is required to have one or more performance goals for each FGPG. Continuing to toward the right, OMB is required to conduct a review of progress with the federal government priority goal's lead official each quarter. Finally, OMB is required to post the most recent quarterly results that were achieved for FGPG 2.

At the agency level, Figure 2 illustrates that each Agency Strategic Plan (graphic at lower left) is required to describe how any of the agency's general goals or objectives may contribute to federal government priority goals. In turn, an Agency Performance Plan is required to describe how the agency's own performance goals, such as the circled "Performance Goal 2," contribute to the agency's general goals in the Agency Strategic Plan. The APP also is required to describe how agency-level performance goals contribute to the executive branch-level federal government performance goals in the Federal Government Performance Plan. If an agency has a performance goal that also is designated as an agency priority goal (e.g., "APG 2"), GPRAMA requires the agency to review quarterly progress with the relevant goal leader. Finally, the law requires OMB and agencies to post online the most recent quarterly results for each agency priority goal.

The ways in which OMB and agencies present information to Congress in these products and processes may vary over time. GPRAMA establishes minimum expectations in law, however.

POTENTIAL IMPLICATIONS AND ISSUES FOR CONGRESS

Some Potential Implications

Depending on how GPRAMA's changes are implemented, the law may have significant implications. To highlight a few, GPRAMA brings additional attention to policy implementation and oversight in several ways. For example, GPRA 1993 focused on annual plans that were used to support the President's budget proposal. These plans were not required to be revised to reflect congressional action. By contrast, GPRAMA adds a requirement that effectively requires the Agency Performance Plans to be updated to reflect this policy making. In quarterly reviews, the law may bring focus to achieving goals during policy implementation, and the performance-related website may facilitate congressional oversight. GPRAMA's requirements for individual officials to be responsible for various management- and performance-related tasks also may provide a convenient means for Congress to interact with agencies about discrete topics.

GPRAMA continues with GPRA 1993's emphasis on goal-setting and performance measurement, with little explicit emphasis on producing or presenting program evaluations. Under GPRA 1993, this sometimes could leave unclear how well programs themselves were performing, why, and what might be done in response.[37] For example, achievement or non-achievement of a goal might be driven by "external" factors other than the program, and measurement of goal achievement may reveal little information that is actionable for an agency, Congress, or the President. At the same time, GPRAMA also brings more attention to goal-setting and performance in areas that cut across federal programs and agencies. As shown in Figure 2, the law established a new set of executive branch-wide products and processes. In addition, nearly 20 provisions in GPRAMA relate to the concept of crosscutting policy areas, where multiple agencies, programs, regulations, delivery partners, and other policy tools may "contribute" to the accomplishment of a goal or desired outcome. Several provisions require assessments of whether activities that cut across these boundaries are contributing toward achievement of the same goal. GPRAMA does not specify how such assessments are to be made or presented to Congress. Nevertheless, agencies and OMB might use program evaluations or "logic modeling" (see Appendix B) to portray and demonstrate these relationships.

In several ways, GPRAMA establishes more specific requirements for agency and OMB interactions with Congress. For example, agency consultations with Congress about Agency Strategic Plans are required to include both majority and minority views from authorizing, appropriations, and oversight committees. In this context, another GPRAMA provision requires consultations with "appropriate" committees to occur every two years. Similarly, when OMB coordinates development of long-term federal government priority goals, GPRAMA requires OMB to consult "periodically" with the majorities and minorities of several specific committees. To provide some accountability with regard to consultations, GPRAMA requires reporting in Agency Strategic Plans and on the OMB website regarding how (or whether) congressional views and suggestions were incorporated into certain kinds of goals.

At the same time, it remains to be seen if GPRAMA could have any implications for the working relationships and the power relationships among Congress, agencies, OMB, the President, and the public. To illustrate, the OMB website has stated that

> [t]he core mission of OMB is to serve the President of the United States in implementing his vision across the Executive Branch.... As the implementation and enforcement arm of Presidential policy government-wide, OMB carries out its mission through five critical processes that are essential to the President's ability to plan and implement his priorities across the Executive Branch.[38]

GPRAMA gives OMB specific statutory authorities that it could attempt to use to influence several products, processes, and institutions.[39] In any of these situations, if a GPRAMA product or process were perceived as reflecting primarily the President's policy preferences or assessing performance in a way that does not reflect underlying statute or congressional intent, some observers might view the product or process as less credible or useful. Similarly, GPRAMA aligns or re-aligns numerous products and processes according to presidential terms and budget proposals. As a consequence, it arguably remains to be seen whether GPRAMA's authorities could be used to alter the responsiveness of agencies to Congress and congressional intent. For example, in spite of more specific consultation requirements, it might become more difficult for Congress to influence agencies' goal-setting in Agency Strategic Plans. Under GPRAMA, all agencies probably will submit draft ASPs to OMB for clearance at the same time, in the first year of a new President's term.[40] This is a time when the President traditionally attempts to influence agencies to adopt and implement his or her policy agenda.[41] As a consequence, OMB's ability to influence or direct the choices of agencies and the information that they present may be enhanced in comparison with GPRA 1993.[42]

GPRAMA's more specific requirements for congressional consultations about ASPs and priority goals, along with transparency from the OMB performance website, also could affect working and power relationships. For example, it remains to be seen whether congressional consultations might mitigate any of the possibilities discussed above, create enhanced opportunities for Congress to influence the choices of agencies, or foster congressional-executive collaboration and compromise.

Potential Issues for Congress

With these and other potential implications in mind, the bullets below highlight more specific issues for Congress that might arise during implementation of GPRAMA. Each bullet also includes questions that might be considered.

- **Congressional consultations and defining "success."** GPRAMA requires agencies and OMB to consult with Congress regarding Agency Strategic Plans, federal government priority goals, and agency submissions of plans and reports to Congress. Committees also might consider asserting broader prerogatives to interact with or direct agencies. In these contexts, have meaningful consultations occurred with relevant committees and Members? Did the consultations occur during formulation of the plans, goals, and proposals, or only after the fact? Are agencies being responsive to committees of jurisdiction? Do committees and Members agree with the way in which agencies or OMB are defining what constitutes a "program," as this is required to be portrayed on the OMB performance website by October 2012? How might committees and Members engage on these topics effectively? Do goals and objectives reflect current law and congressional intent? Does Congress agree with the designation of certain goals as being priority goals? Are plans and goals well formulated and coordinated?
- **Agency and OMB representations about performance.** By design, GPRAMA requires many products to be submitted to Congress to inform its policy deliberations. If the products are to be considered useful to Congress and the public, one input to perceptions of usefulness may be whether the products are perceived as making credible, unbiased representations about how well agencies and programs are performing. How credible are these representations? For a program or agency, is "success" being defined appropriately? Are credible and appropriate methods of policy analysis, measurement, and evaluation being used? What resources and tools might Congress draw upon, including from its support agencies and the public, to scrutinize any "evidence" that is presented? What are the policy implications of available evidence and analyses?
- **Oversight, transparency, and public participation.** Congress oftentimes relies on transparency and public participation to help it

conduct oversight of policy development and implementation within agencies and OMB. Oversight findings may generate interest in subsequent lawmaking or other legislative activity. What have been the recent activities of Performance Improvement Officers and the Performance Improvement Council? Are they functioning effectively? What is happening during quarterly reviews? Are agencies and OMB focusing on learning and improvement in addition to goal achievement? Is the OMB performance website providing the required information? If a goal is removed from the website, or if a goal's target is revised, will the website retain any record of the previous goal or target?[43] Might it be worthwhile to communicate informally with a goal leader or other official who is responsible for a topic under GPRAMA, or more formally invite the official to testify at a hearing? Are non-federal stakeholders being consulted by agencies in the development of Agency Strategic Plans? What are stakeholders' views about agencies' goals? Are OMB and agencies consulting effectively with Congress about the potential elimination of requirements to submit plans and reports to Congress? Is GPRAMA being implemented in a way that helps agency program managers and front-line staff without creating perverse incentives for organizations and individuals?[44]

- **Crosscutting policy areas.** Congress and observers have expressed interest in policy areas that cut across agency and programmatic boundaries. In these areas, more than one agency or program may collaborate and contribute toward desired policy outcomes or, conversely, duplicate effort. For example, GPRAMA requires OMB to include information on its performance website about each agency program and how the program contributes to one or more of the agency's goals. GAO is separately required to report annually on programs, agencies, and initiatives with "duplicative goals and activities."[45] Most of GAO's March 2011 findings cited "potential" fragmentation, overlap, or duplication, and GAO oftentimes recommended further analysis or enhanced coordination. Are agencies and OMB using their scarce analytical resources effectively to coordinate efforts and identify and exploit potential efficiencies? Are agencies and OMB using appropriate tools to conduct these analyses, potentially including evaluations and logic modeling? Are there implications for coordination across congressional committees?

- **GPRAMA's design and implementation**. Compared to the four-year phase-in period for GPRA 1993, the phase-in period for GPRAMA before full implementation is fairly short. Answers to specific questions posed above about the implementation of GPRAMA may raise broader questions about how well the law is designed and how well it is being implemented by OMB or specific agencies. In that light, how well is GPRAMA serving Congress's needs? How well is it serving the needs of agency personnel, the President, and the public? Are agencies and OMB adequately complying with the act? Are agencies and OMB using the act in way that promotes improvement and learning in addition to accountability? Do agencies have the necessary capacity—including staff, skills, technology, and funding—to implement the law's numerous and detailed requirements? In response to any of these topics, and if a problem were perceived, what options might be considered to enhance the law's design or implementation?

APPENDIX A. ACRONYMS

This table lists acronyms that are used in this report. For some entries, text that is located inside parentheses indicates when an acronym is associated with implementation of GPRAMA, GPRA 1993, another law, or a presidential initiative. For acronyms associated with a particular President, the table indicates the relevant administration. In practice, some terms and corresponding acronyms have been used that do not mirror the precise language from underlying statutes. In Appendix B, a glossary provides more information about these cases.

APG	Agency Priority Goal (GPRAMA)
APP	Agency Performance Plan (GPRAMA) or Annual Performance Plan (GPRA 1993)
APR	Annual Performance Report (non-statutory term associated with GPRAMA and GPRA 1993)
APU	Annual Performance Update (GPRAMA)
ASP	Agency Strategic Plan (GPRAMA)
CFO	Chief Financial Officer (CFO Act)
CHCO	Chief Human Capital Officer (P.L. 107-296)

CFO Act	Chief Financial Officers Act of 1990 (P.L. 101-576)
COO	Chief Operating Officer (GPRAMA)
DDM	Deputy Director for Management (of the Office of Management and Budget)
EOP	Executive Office of the President
FGPG	Federal Government Priority Goal (GPRAMA)
FGPP	Federal Government Performance Plan (GPRAMA)
FY	Fiscal Year
GAO	Government Accountability Office (previously General Accounting Office)
GPRA 1993	Government Performance and Results Act of 1993 (P.L. 103-62)
GPRAMA	GPRA Modernization Act of 2010 (P.L. 111-352)
HPPG	High Priority Performance Goal (Barack Obama Administration)
OMB	Office of Management and Budget (in the Executive Office of the President)
OPM	Office of Personnel Management
PAR	Performance and Accountability Report (RCA, GPRA 1993, and GPRAMA)
PART	Program Assessment Rating Tool (George W. Bush Administration)
PBP	President's Budget Proposal (Budget and Accounting Act, 1921; codified at 31 U.S.C. §1105)
PIC	Performance Improvement Council (GPRAMA and George W. Bush Administration)
PIO	Performance Improvement Officer (GPRAMA and George W. Bush Administration)
PPR	Program Performance Report (GPRA 1993)
RCA	Reports Consolidation Act of 2000 (P.L. 106-531)
SP	Strategic Plan (GPRA 1993)

APPENDIX B. GLOSSARY OF TERMS

Government processes oftentimes involve specialized terms. The federal budget process, for example, has evolved to a level of complexity where participants in the process often perceive a need for glossaries and guides.[46] GPRAMA similarly establishes an elaborate framework of products and processes that focus on government performance. In doing so, the law uses terms that are interrelated and sometimes technical in nature.[47] Notably, the designs and legislative histories of GPRA 1993 and GPRAMA indicate Congress's intention for Congress itself, along with agencies, the President, non-federal stakeholders, and the broader public, to be consumers of the laws' products and to actively participate in the laws' processes for managing performance of the government.[48] To assist with navigating through GPRAMA's varied products and processes, this glossary provides capsule summaries and statutory citations for related terms.[49] In each entry, when a term is included that also is listed elsewhere in the glossary, the term is written in italics the first time it is used.

Glossary

agency	GPRAMA imposes requirements on certain federal agencies. The act's use of the term "agency" determines which agencies are covered by these requirements. In GPRAMA, the term is defined as an "executive agency" under 5 U.S.C. §105. This definition includes most executive branch departments and agencies but explicitly does not include the Central Intelligence Agency, the Government Accountability Office, the United States Postal Service, and the Postal Regulatory Commission. (GPRAMA, Section 3, 31 U.S.C. §1115(h)(1); and Section 2, 5 U.S.C. §306(f).) GPRA 1993 used the same definition.
Agency Performance Plan (APP)	Under GPRAMA, an agency-level, two-year plan that an agency is required to submit annually according to the same schedule as the *President's budget proposal.* (GPRAMA, Section 3, 31 U.S.C. §1115(b).) The plan includes performance goals for the next fiscal year and updates *performance goals* for the current fiscal year. In addition, GPRAMA requires the plan to describe how the performance goals contribute to *general goals and objectives* in an *Agency Strategic Plan* and to any of the *federal government performance goals* that are in the *Federal Government Performance Plan.* The Agency Performance Plan also is required to contain information

about how performance goals are to be achieved, establish "balanced sets" of *performance indicators*, address *major management challenges*, and identify "low-priority" *program activities*. A classified appendix may be submitted to cover any portion of an Agency Performance Plan that by executive order is both authorized to be kept secret and properly classified. GPRAMA states that the drafting of an APP is considered to be *inherently governmental*, which means that this activity may not be contracted out. The requirement for an Agency Performance Plan replaced the GPRA 1993 requirement for an *Annual Performance Plan*.

Agency Performance Update (APU) GPRAMA requires that an "update on agency performance" be made available annually on the agency's public website. (GPRAMA, Section 4, 31 U.S.C. §1116.) For ease of reference, this report refers to the product as an Agency Performance Update (APU). The APU is required to provide, among other things, comparisons of *performance goals* from the two-year *Agency Performance Plan* with actual performance. It could be argued that the authors of the legislation intended for the APU to be made available no later than 150 days after the end of the fiscal year,[50] which was the timing requirement for GPRA 1993's *Program Performance Report* (PPR). If an APU includes any *program activity* or information that by executive order is both authorized to be kept secret and properly classified, an agency head is required to make the information available in a classified appendix to the Agency Performance Plan. GPRAMA states that the drafting of an APU is considered to be *inherently governmental*, which means that this activity may not be contracted out. The requirement for the APU replaced the GPRA 1993 requirement for a PPR. In practice, OMB sometimes has called the APU and PPR by a different name: *Annual Performance Report*. In compliance with the *Reports Consolidation Act of 2000*, OMB has said administratively that agencies may comply with the requirement to publish the APU by either including the APU with along with the agency's congressional budget justification (in February of each year, to accompany the *President's budget proposal*) or, if an agency produces a *Performance and Accountability Report* (PAR), including the APU along with the PAR (typically due by November 15, 45 days after the end of an agency's fiscal year).[51]

agency priority goal (APG) Under GPRAMA, a small subset of agency-level *performance goals* from an agency's Agency *Performance Plan* may be given this additional designation. (GPRAMA, Section 5, 31 U.S.C. §1120(b).) Agency heads are required to identify agency priority goals (APGs) every two years, but OMB is authorized to deviate from this requirement and to specify the manner and timing of how agency priority goals are to be identified. APGs are required to reflect the "highest priorities of the agency" as determined by the agency head, and as informed by *federal government priority goals* and congressional consultations regarding an *Agency Strategic Plan*. Each APG is required to have a corresponding agency official, or *goal leader*, who is responsible for achieving the goal. OMB determines the total number of APGs across the government and also for each agency. With establishment of APGs and *quarterly priority progress reviews*, GPRAMA enacted into law a framework similar to the Obama Administration's initiative to pursue *high-priority performance goals*. If an APG includes any *program activity* or information that by executive order is both authorized to be kept secret and properly classified, an agency head is required to make the information available in a classified appendix to the Agency Performance Plan. GPRAMA states that the development of an APG is considered to be *inherently governmental*, which means that this activity may not be contracted out.

agency quarterly Under GPRAMA, a "review" that an agency head and *Chief Operating Officer* conduct with a minimum

priority progress review frequency of every three months for each *agency priority goal.* (GPRAMA, Section 6, 31 U.S.C. §1121(b).) The review is required to include a *goal leader* and to be supported by the agency's *Performance Improvement Officer.* The agency head and Chief Operating Officer are further required to coordinate with personnel within and outside the agency who contribute to the accomplishment of each agency priority goal. Several assessments are required to take place in this context. GPRAMA specifies no product or transparency requirement for the quarterly reviews themselves. Under the Obama Administration's *high-priority performance goal* initiative, OMB conducted similarly structured quarterly reviews as in-person meetings.

Agency Strategic Plan (ASP) Under GPRAMA, an agency-level, four-year plan that an agency is required to submit every four years at the beginning of the second year of each presidential term and on the same schedule as the *President's budget proposal.* (GPRAMA, Section 2, 5 U.S.C. §306.) The plan is required to contain, among other things, *general goals and objectives* for the major functions and operations of the agency, a description of how the goals and objectives contribute to *federal government priority goals*, and a description of how the goals and objectives incorporate views and suggestions obtained through certain congressional consultations. When an agency is developing or adjusting its Agency Strategic Plan, GPRAMA requires the agency to consult with Congress, including majority and minority views from the "appropriate" authorizing, appropriations, and oversight committees, and also to solicit and consider the views and suggestions of entities affected by or interested in the plan. Regardless of whether the plan is revised during a President's term, an agency also is required to consult with "appropriate" committees every two years. GPRAMA states that the drafting of an Agency Strategic Plan is considered to be *inherently governmental*, which means that this activity may not be contracted out. The requirement for this plan replaced the GPRA 1993

	requirement for a *Strategic Plan*.
Annual Performance Plan (APP)	No longer current law. An agency-level, annually submitted, one-year plan that was required by GPRA 1993. GPRAMA replaced the requirements for this plan with expanded requirements for an *Agency Performance Plan*.
Annual Performance Report (APR)	See *Program Performance Report and Agency Performance Update*.
Chief Human Capital Officer (CHCO)	A statutorily established position that GPRAMA requires to prepare a portion of the *Agency Performance Plan*. The Chief Human Capital Officer (CHCO) is required to prepare the APP's description of how *performance goals* are to be achieved, including "the operation processes, training, skills and technology, and the human, capital, information, and other resources and strategies required to meet those performance goals" (GPRAMA, Section 3; 31 U.S.C. §1115(b)(5)(A) and §1115(g).) GPRA 1993 contained the same requirement after it was amended in 2002. The Homeland Security Act of 2002 (P.L. 107-296, Title XIII; 116 Stat. 2135, at 2289) established CHCOs in agencies widely known as the "CFO Act agencies."[52]
Chief Operating Officer (COO)	Under GPRAMA, a designation that is given to the deputy head of an agency or an equivalent position. (GPRAMA, Section 8, 31 U.S.C. §1123.) The law enumerates several duties for a Chief Operating Officer (COO), including responsibility for improving the management and performance of the agency and assisting the agency head in complying with GPRAMA's requirements. An agency's *Performance Improvement Officer* is required to report directly to the COO.
crosscutting	Under GPRAMA, an adjective that is defined as describing something that cuts across organizational and agency boundaries, such as a policy or goal. (GPRAMA, Section 3; 31 U.S.C. §1115(h)(2).) The law requires OMB to identify *major management challenges* that are government-wide or crosscutting in nature in the

	Federal Government Performance Plan. In addition, for the *federal government priority goals*, OMB is required to develop *outcome*-oriented goals covering a limited number of crosscutting policy areas. Nearly 20 provisions in GPRAMA relate to the concept of crosscutting policy areas, because the provisions refer to the possibility of multiple agencies, activities, delivery partners, and policy tools "contributing" to the accomplishment of a goal or desired outcome. Many provisions require assessments of whether activities that cut across organizational boundaries are contributing toward achievement of the same goal. GPRAMA does not specify how such assessments are to be made. In practice, agencies may use a method called logic modeling to comply with these provisions, and stakeholders may use *logic modeling* to assess agencies' representations.
customer service measure	Under GPRAMA, defined as an assessment of service delivery to a customer, client, citizen, or other recipient, which "can include an assessment of quality, timeliness, and satisfaction among other factors" (GPRAMA, Section 3, 31 U.S.C. §1115(h)(3).) See also *performance indicator* in this glossary.
Deputy Director for Management (DDM)	A statutorily established OMB position that is subject to Senate confirmation. The OMB Deputy Director for Management (DDM) position was established by the Chief Financial Officers Act of 1990 (P.L. 101-576), with many statutory functions codified at 31 U.S.C. §503. The DDM is responsible for establishing general management policies for executive agencies across a variety of mission-support functions like procurement and financial management, subject to the direction and approval of the Director of OMB. GPRAMA gives authority to OMB's DDM to determine the agenda and direct the work of the *Performance Improvement Council*, which is composed of agency *Performance Improvement Officers*.
efficiency measure	Under GPRAMA, defined as a ratio of a program activity's inputs, like costs or hours worked, to either its

outputs, such as amount or products or services delivered, or to its outcomes, such as the desired results of a program. (GPRAMA, Section 3, 31 U.S.C. §1115(h)(4).) See also *performance indicator* in this glossary.

evidence GPRAMA does not define the term "evidence." Nevertheless, GPRAMA requires an agency to provide evidence for certain purposes. Specifically, the *Agency Performance Plan* that accompanies the agency's portion of the *President's budget proposal* is required to "identify low-priority program activities based on an analysis of their contribution to the mission and goals of the agency and include an evidence-based justification for designating a program activity as low priority." (GPRAMA, Section 3, 31 U.S.C. §1115(b)(10).) In practice, definitions of what constitutes evidence for budgetary decision making have varied markedly and often have been controversial.[53] Definitions of what constitutes evidence for learning and decisions about the future have drawn from at least three categories of considerations: (1) retrospective *program evaluations* and *performance measurements*, (2) prospective policy analyses such as risk assessment and forecasting, and (3) current-day conceptions of ethics, values, and risk preference. When the definition of success for a program is contested—with different views on how to judge what constitutes good performance—even widespread consensus on how to interpret evaluations, measurements and policy analyses still may yield disagreements about priorities and future decisions. In some cases, "evidence" may be viewed through additional lenses of values, ethics, and risk preference. Observations like these suggest that when an advocate for a proposal uses an implicit or explicit definition of evidence, there is a chance that the definition may be selective or may not be politically neutral.

external factors Under GPRAMA, agencies are required to identify key factors external to the agency and beyond its control that could significantly affect whether certain goals are

	achieved. Similar requirements were imposed under GPRA 1993, and these factors came to be known as "external factors." Under GPRAMA, agencies are required to identify in an *Agency Strategic Plan* the external factors that correspond to *general goals and objectives*. Agencies also are required to identify on the GPRAMA-required OMB website the external factors that correspond to *agency priority goals*.
federal government performance goal	See *performance goal* in this glossary.
federal government performance indicator	See *performance indicator* in this glossary.
Federal Government Performance Plan (FGPP)	Under GPRAMA, an executive branch-wide, two-year plan that OMB is required to submit to Congress annually with the *President's budget proposal*. (GPRAMA, Section 3, 31 U.S.C. §1115(a).) The plan establishes *federal government performance goals* for the next fiscal year and updates federal government performance goals for the current fiscal year. One or more of these federal government performance goals are required to be established for each *federal government priority goal*. For each federal government performance goal, the Federal Government Performance Plan (FGPP) is required to provide more detailed information, including "common" *federal government performance indicators*. The Senate committee report accompanying the legislation said these indicators would "measure and assess progress across agencies toward shared goals."[54] GPRAMA states that the drafting of a FGPP is considered to be *inherently governmental*, which means that this activity may not be contracted out. Before enactment of GPRAMA, GPRA 1993 required the President to submit to Congress an annual FGPP, but did not specify the plan's contents. (GPRA 1993, Section 4(a), 31 U.S.C. §1105(a).) During that time, OMB

considered the President's budget proposal to satisfy the GPRA 1993 requirement for a FGPP.

federal government priority goal (FGPG) Under GPRAMA, goals that are developed and updated by OMB with a minimum frequency of every four years and made available concurrently with the *President's budget proposal* at the beginning of the second year of a President's term. (GPRAMA, Section 5, 31 U.S.C. §1120(a).) The federal government priority goals (FGPGs) are required to be long-term in nature and are required to include at least two types of goals: *outcome*-oriented goals that cover a limited number of *crosscutting* policy areas, and goals for management improvements across the federal government in areas like financial management and procurement. For every FGPG, one or more *federal government performance goals* are required to be established in the annually submitted *Federal Government Performance Plan*. An *Agency Strategic Plan* is required to describe how any of the agency's *general goals and objectives* contribute to FGPGs. When OMB is developing or adjusting these goals, GPRAMA requires OMB to consult with the majority and minority of specific committees—House and Senate Committees on Appropriations, House and Senate Committees on the Budget, Senate Committee on Homeland Security and Governmental Affairs, House Committee on Oversight and Government Reform, Senate Committee on Finance, and House Committee on Ways and Means—plus other committees "as determined appropriate." GPRAMA includes another provision that requires OMB to consult with "the appropriate" committees every two years, presumably about FGPGs. GPRAMA states that the development of a FGPG is considered to be *inherently governmental*, which means that this activity may not be contracted out.

general goals and objectives Under GPRAMA, goals and objectives that are specified in an *Agency Strategic Plan* and which correspond to an agency's major functions and operations. (GPRAMA, Section 2, 5 U.S.C. §306.) The law requires that these goals and objectives include *outcome*-oriented goals, but

	not exclusively. In addition, an Agency Strategic Plan is required to describe, among other things, how any of these goals contribute to *federal government priority goals* and how the goals and objectives incorporate congressional views and suggestions.
goal leader	Under GPRAMA, an *Agency Performance Plan* is required to identify agency officials with this designation who are responsible for the achievement of each agency-level *performance goal*. (GPRAMA, Section 3, 31 U.S.C. §1115(b)(5)(E).) In another provision, an agency is required to have an agency official with this designation who is responsible for the achievement of each *agency priority goal*. (GPRAMA, Section 5, 5 U.S.C. §1120(b)(1)(C).) Other provisions in GPRAMA require the identification of government officials with responsibility for certain kinds of goals, but do not use the term "goal leader." In the case of the *Federal Government Performance Plan*, each *federal government performance goal* is required to have a corresponding "lead Government official." (GPRAMA, Section 3, 31 U.S.C. §1115(a)(3).) In an Agency Performance Plan, an agency is required to identify the "agency official" who is responsible for resolving *major management challenges*. (GPRAMA, Section 3, 31 U.S.C. §1115(b)(9)(C).) When an agency does not meet its performance goals and in response develops a *Performance Improvement Plan*, an agency is required to designate a "senior official" to oversee performance improvement strategies for each unmet goal. (GPRAMA, Section 4, 31 U.S.C. §1116(g).)
high priority performance goal (HPPG)	A goal established under one of the Obama Administration's government performance-related initiatives. The initiative began in 2009. It resulted in the release of high-priority performance goals (HPPGs) in February 2010 with the FY2011 *President's budget proposal*. OMB guidance for the HPPG initiative required agencies to develop goals to, among other things, be achievable in 12-24 months; highly valued by the public or reflecting achievement of agency missions;

authorized by law; and sufficiently funded by Congress in order to be achieved. OMB later began to hold quarterly, in-person meetings with agency officials to review progress against the HPPGs. GPRAMA enacted aspects of this initiative into law through requirements for *priority goals and quarterly priority progress reviews*.

inherently governmental A term that refers to situations when a function or activity must be performed only by government employees as a matter of federal law and policy. Inherently governmental functions may not be contracted out. Like GPRA 1993, GPRAMA states that some functions and activities are considered to be inherently governmental. Under GPRAMA, these functions and activities include (1) the drafting of *Agency Strategic Plans, the Federal Government Performance Plan, Agency Performance Plans, and Agency Performance Updates*; and (2) the development of *federal government priority goals and agency priority goals*.

input measure A measurement of the resources that are used to undertake activities, produce *outputs*, and influence *outcomes*. Some types of resources include funding, personnel, and capital investments such as information technology. See also *logic model*.

logic model A logic model shows how multiple *inputs*, activities, and *outputs* in one or more agencies and delivery partners relate to each other and are expected to influence *outcomes*.[55] In this way, logic models may assist with understanding the relationships among activities and policy outcomes and assessing how well programs work. Logic modeling may be utilized to address several requirements in GPRAMA. The law contains nearly 20 provisions that refer to the prospect of multiple agencies, activities, delivery partners, and policy tools "contributing" to the accomplishment of a goal or desired outcome. Some provisions require assessments of whether these *crosscutting* activities are contributing toward achievement of the same goal. GPRAMA does

	not specify how such assessments are to be made. In practice, logic models may be used in several ways to assess how multiple agencies and delivery partners contribute toward achievement of an outcome. These include assessing performance, setting goals, identifying potential program overlap and duplication, and coordinating activities in crosscutting policy areas. Logic models also may be used to help assess performance when outcomes are driven substantially by *external factors*. By focusing on how measurable inputs, activities, and outputs relate to an outcome, a logic model also may be used by an agency or stakeholder to integrate *performance measurement* and *program evaluation*.[56]
major management challenge	Under GPRAMA, defined as programs or management functions, within or across agencies, that have greater vulnerability to waste, fraud, abuse, and mismanagement, where a failure to perform well could seriously affect the ability of an agency or the government to achieve its mission or goals. GPRAMA's definition explicitly cites issues identified by GAO as high-risk or identified by an inspector general as examples of major management challenges. (GPRAMA, Section 3, 31 U.S.C. §1115(h)(5).) GPRAMA requires that major management challenges be addressed in certain ways in *Agency Performance Plans* and the *Federal Government Performance Plan*. In an Agency Performance Plan, an agency is required to identify the "agency official" who is responsible for resolving these challenges. (GPRAMA, Section 3, 31 U.S.C. §1115(b)(9)(C).)
milestone	Under GPRAMA, defined as a scheduled event signifying the completion of a major deliverable or a set of related deliverables or a phase of work. (GPRAMA, Section 3, 31 U.S.C. §1115(h)(6).) The law requires milestones to be used in the *Federal Government Performance Plan* in two contexts: when describing plans to address *major management challenges* that are government-wide or *crosscutting* in nature; and

quarterly milestones for unstated purposes, but possibly in reference to *federal government performance goals.* GPRAMA also requires milestones to be used in an *Agency Performance Plan* when describing how *performance goals* are to be achieved and how *major management challenges* that the agency faces are to be resolved. Finally, if OMB determines that an agency has not met a performance goal for one fiscal year, GPRAMA requires the agency to submit a *Performance Improvement Plan* to OMB, with milestones, for each unmet goal. See also *OMB Reports on Unmet Goals* in this glossary.

OMB performance website Under GPRAMA, a website that OMB is required to operate and, for certain information, update with a minimum quarterly frequency. The website is required to provide detailed information about agency *programs, agency priority goals*, and *federal government priority goals*; annually make information available from the *Federal Government Performance Plan*; and post *Agency Strategic Plans, Agency Performance Plans*, and *Agency Performance Updates*. Notably, the website is required to describe how both kinds of priority goals incorporate views and suggestions obtained through certain congressional consultations. (GPRAMA; Section 3, 31 U.S.C. §1115(a); Section 5, 31 U.S.C. §1120(a)(5); Section 7, 31 U.S.C. §1122; and Section 10, 31 U.S.C. §1115 note.) This requirement appears to be modeled in part on the Obama Administration's Performance.gov website.

OMB quarterly priority progress review Under GPRAMA, a "review" that OMB conducts with a minimum frequency of every three months for each *federal government priority goal*. (GPRAMA, Section 6, 31 U.S.C. §1121(a).) The review is required to include a "lead government official" plus officials from agencies, organizations, and *program activities* that contribute to accomplishment of the federal government priority goal, and to be supported by the *Performance Improvement Council*. Several assessments are required to take place in this context. GPRAMA does not specifically require the identification of a lead official for each federal government priority goal. As a result, it is not clear how the lead government official for a federal government priority goal will be identified. (GPRAMA requires a *Federal Government Performance Plan* to identify a lead government official for each *federal government performance goal.*) GPRAMA specifies no product or transparency requirement for the quarterly reviews themselves. Under the Obama Administration's *high-priority performance goal* initiative, OMB conducted similarly structured quarterly reviews as in-person meetings.

OMB and Agency Reports and Plans on Unmet Goals

Under GPRAMA, a variety of annual reporting requirements that focus on whether an agency is meeting *performance goals* in its *Agency Performance Plan.* (GPRAMA, Section 6, 31 U.S.C. §§1116(f), 1116(h), and 1116(i).) OMB is required to submit a report annually on "unmet goals" to each agency, two congressional committees, and GAO. If OMB determines that an agency's *programs* or activities have not met performance goals for one fiscal year, an agency is required to submit a *Performance Improvement Plan* to OMB. If OMB determines that an agency's programs or activities have unmet performance goals for either two or three consecutive fiscal years, the agency and OMB, respectively, have further reporting requirements to Congress. When OMB determines that performance goal remains unmet for two consecutive years, the agency's head is required to submit to Congress a description of what actions "the Administration" will take to improve performance, including legislative proposals and the obligation of additional funding for an amount determined by OMB. In this situation, GPRAMA indicates that an agency head shall use any reprogramming or transfer authority available to it. When OMB determines that a performance goal remains unmet for three consecutive years, GPRAMA requires OMB to submit recommendations to improve performance within 60 days, including reauthorization

	proposals, other statutory changes, planned actions, and identification of a program for termination or reduction in the *President's budget proposal.*
outcome measure	Under GPRAMA, defined as an assessment of the results of a *program activity* compared to its intended purpose. (GPRAMA, Section 3, 31 U.S.C. §1115(h)(7).) This term also was defined by GPRA 1993, and the definition was carried forward by GPRAMA without change. See also *performance indicator* and *logic model* in this glossary.
output measure	Under GPRAMA, defined as the tabulation, calculation, or recording of activity or effort that can be expressed in a quantitative or qualitative manner. (GPRAMA, Section 3, 31 U.S.C. §1115(h)(8).) This term also was defined by GPRA 1993, and the definition was carried forward by GPRAMA without change. See also *performance indicator* and *logic model* in this glossary.
Performance and Accountability Report (PAR)	The Reports Consolidation Act of 2000 (RCA, P.L. 106-531) permitted an agency, with OMB concurrence, to package its GPRA 1993-required *Annual Performance Report* together with certain financial statements and reports. If an agency did so, the consolidated document was to be called a Performance and Accountability Report (PAR). Because GPRAMA did not modify this statutory flexibility (31 U.S.C. §3516), the applicable provision appears to allow an agency's GPRAMA-required *Agency Performance Update* to be similarly consolidated. OMB requires PARs to be submitted to Congress no later than 45 calendar days after the end of an agency's fiscal year (e.g., November 15), and draft PARs be submitted to OMB for clearance at least 10 working days before then.
performance goal	Under GPRAMA, defined as a target level of performance expressed as a tangible, measurable objective, against which actual achievement can be compared. This may include a goal expressed as a quantitative standard, value, or rate. (GPRAMA, Section 3, 31 U.S.C. §1115(h)(9).) This term also was defined by GPRA 1993, and the definition was carried forward

by GPRAMA without change. Under GPRAMA, performance goals come in two general categories. First, agency-level "performance goals" are required to be established in an *Agency Performance Plan* (31 U.S.C. §1115(b)(1) and §1115(b)(9)(B)). A small subset of these agency-level performance goals are required to be identified as *agency priority goals* (APG). An agency is required to identify *goal leaders* who are responsible for the achievement of each agency-level performance goal and each APG. In the second category, *federal government performance goals* (FGPGs) are required to be established in the *Federal Government Performance Plan* (31 U.S.C. §1115(a)(1)). For each *federal government priority goal*, OMB is required to establish one or more federal government performance goals (31 U.S.C. §1115(a)(1) and 31 U.S.C. §1120(a)). Each federal government performance goal is required to have a corresponding "lead Government official." In the context of agency-level performance goals, an agency may determine in consultation with OMB that it is not feasible to express a performance goal in an "objective, quantifiable, and measurable form." In such cases, OMB may authorize an "alternative form" of performance goal that includes descriptive statements of a "successful" program and "minimally effective" program (31 U.S.C. §1115(c)).

Performance Improvement Council (PIC)

Under GPRAMA, an interagency council of *Performance Improvement Officers*. (GPRAMA, Section 9, 31 U.S.C. §1124(b).) OMB directly controls the Performance Improvement Council (PIC) through the chairpersonship of OMB's *Deputy Director for Management* (DDM). OMB's DDM leads the PIC, determines its agenda, and directs its work. The council consists of the OMB DDM; Performance Improvement Officers (PIOs) from the 24 largest executive branch agencies, also known as the "CFO Act agencies";[57] and other individuals and Performance Improvement Officers as determined by the DDM. The PIC's duties mainly focus on assisting OMB and providing recommendations to the Director of OMB and the President. Among other things, these duties include assisting the Director of OMB in implementing GPRAMA's provisions related to *federal government priority goals*. OMB may require each agency with a PIO member of the PIC to provide up to two "personnel authorizations" to serve at the direction of OMB's DDM. OMB could use this authority to control a staff of 48 or more agency personnel (24 CFO Act agencies multiplied by two staff from each agency). GPRAMA does not explicitly provide for transparency outside the executive branch into the PIC's activities. The PIC previously had been established by E.O. 13450,[58] which GPRAMA appeared to draw upon. Under the executive order, the PIC operated with little transparency outside the executive branch since the beginning of its activities in January 2008.

Performance Improvement Officer (PIO) Under GPRAMA, a designation that is given to a career or politically appointed "senior executive" at an agency. (GPRAMA, Section 9, 31 U.S.C. §1124(a).) The Performance Improvement Officer (PIO) is required to report directly to the agency's Chief Operating Officer. The law provides little independent authority to a PIO and enumerates mainly advisory duties, including advising the agency head and Chief Operating Officer on goal-setting, measurement, and reviewing progress toward *agency priority goals*. GPRAMA provides that the PIOs at the largest executive branch agencies are members of the *Performance Improvement Council*, an interagency group that is led by OMB's *Deputy Director for Management*. The Deputy Director for Management also may designate other PIOs as members of the council. GPRAMA does not explicitly provide for transparency outside the executive branch into PIOs' activities. PIOs previously had been established by E.O. 13450, which GPRAMA appeared to draw upon. Under the executive order, PIOs operated with little transparency outside the executive branch since the beginning of their activities in January 2008.

Performance Improvement Plan (PIP) Under GPRAMA, a plan that an agency must submit to OMB if the agency's programs or activities have not met *performance goals* in the *Agency Performance Plan* for one fiscal year, as determined by OMB. (GPRAMA, Section 6, 31 U.S.C. §1116(g).) In this context, an agency is required to designate a "senior official" to oversee performance improvement strategies for each unmet goal. (GPRAMA, Section 4, 31 U.S.C. §1116(g).) See also *OMB and Agency Reports and Plans on Unmet Goals.*

performance indicator Under GPRAMA, defined as a particular value or characteristic used to measure *output* or *outcome.* (GPRAMA, Section 3, 31 U.S.C. §1115(h)(10).) This term also was defined by GPRA 1993, and the definition was carried forward by GPRAMA without change. GPRAMA contemplates agency-level performance indicators and federal-government-level performance indicators. In the first case, the law's requirement for an *Agency Performance Plan* requires that a "balanced set" of performance indicators be established for each *performance goal*. Each set is to include, as appropriate, *customer service*, *efficiency*, *output*, and *outcome* indicators. In the second category, GPRAMA requires the *Federal Government Performance Plan* to establish "common" federal government performance indicators for each *federal government performance goal.* The Federal Government Performance Plan also is required to include relevant performance indicators for *major management challenges* that are government-wide or crosscutting in nature. See also *performance measurement* in this glossary.

performance measurement Performance measurement is narrower in focus than *program evaluation* and typically refers to periodic monitoring and reporting of data that are related to government policies and programs. In isolation, performance measurement data often are viewed as managerially useful. However, performance measures, which sometimes are called indicators or metrics, do not necessarily reflect how well a government program or policy is working, because the measures may be significantly driven by *external factors* other than the program or policy.

President's budget proposal (PBP) By law, the President is required to submit to Congress an annual "budget of the United States Government" for the following fiscal year, including some information that is specified in statute, on or after the first Monday in January but not later than the first Monday in February of each year. (31 U.S.C. §1105.) The submission includes consolidated budget proposals for federal agencies and establishments. OMB compiles the proposal on behalf of the President. In this process, an executive branch agency's views about funding needs may be modified by OMB before the proposal is submitted to Congress, in order to reflect the policy preferences of the President.[59] The President's budget proposal also may present information to justify the proposals. Under GPRA 1993, an agency's *Annual Performance Plan* was required to be submitted to OMB along with the agency's original budget proposal, before modification by OMB. GPRAMA considerably expands the number of products that are required to be submitted according to the same schedule as the President's budget proposal, including *Agency Strategic Plans*, *Agency Performance Plans, federal government priority goals, the Federal Government Performance Plan*, and, for FY2013, *agency priority goals*.

presidential list of plans and reports for Congress Under GPRAMA, the President is required to submit annually to Congress a list of plans and reports that agencies produce for Congress that, according to the statute, the agencies "identified for elimination or consolidation because the plans and reports are determined outdated or duplicative of other required plans and reports." (GPRAMA, Section 11, 31 U.S.C. §1105(a)(37) and 31 U.S.C. §1125.) As an input to presidential formulation of this list, agencies are required to submit to OMB, among other things, a list of plans and reports that are labeled as "outdated and duplicative." During the first year of implementation, each agency is required to identify not less than 10% of its plans and reports to Congress as outdated or duplicative.

priority goal See *agency priority goal and federal government priority goal in this glossary.* There is no consensus

program definition for the term "program." Depending on an observer's preference, the term may include any government function, policy, activity, project, initiative, law, tax provision, or group thereof. GPRAMA requires OMB to include information on the *OMB performance website* about each program identified by an agency. The posted information is required to include an identification of how the agency defines the term program. However, agencies are to define the term in a manner consistent with OMB guidance. (GPRAMA, Section 7, 31 U.S.C. §1122(a).)

program activity Under GPRAMA, defined as specific activity or project as listed in the program and financing schedules of the *President's budget proposal.* (GPRAMA, Section 3; 31 U.S.C. §1115(h)(11).) This term also was defined by GPRA 1993, and the definition was carried forward by GPRAMA without change. One or more program activities typically are listed for each appropriation or fund account in the "appendix" volume of the President's budget proposal. In practice, a program activity may represent an aggregation or disaggregation of an agency's *programs*, organizations, and activities that are funded by one appropriations account. GPRAMA requires an Agency Performance Plan to "cover each program activity set forth in the budget [request]."

program evaluation Under GPRAMA, defined as an assessment, through objective measurement and systematic analysis, of the manner and extent to which federal *programs* achieve intended objectives. (GPRAMA, Section 3; 31 U.S.C. §1115(h)(12).) This term also was defined by GPRA 1993, and the definition was carried forward by GPRAMA without change. Program evaluation is broader in scope than *performance measurement*. In practice, program evaluation uses one or more methods to answer questions about how well programs are working, whether they are achieving their objectives or causing unintended consequences, why they are performing as they are, and how they can be improved. It may encompass one or more studies, or may be pursued as an ongoing activity. Like GPRA 1993, GPRAMA focuses primarily on goal-setting and performance measurement, and its requirements regarding program evaluation are limited. GPRAMA requires an *Agency Strategic Plan* to describe the program evaluations used in establishing or revising *general goals and objectives*. The law also requires an ASP to contain a schedule for future program evaluations. An *Agency Performance Update* is required to include summary findings of program evaluations completed during the period covered by the update.

Program Performance Report (PPR) No longer current law. An agency-level, annually submitted, one-year report that was required by GPRA 1993. OMB sometimes called this document an Annual Program Performance Report or *Annual Performance Report* (APR). GPRAMA replaced the requirements for this report with expanded requirements for an "update on agency performance." This report refers to the new product as the *Agency Performance Update*.

quarterly priority progress review See *agency quarterly priority progress review* and *OMB quarterly priority progress review* in this glossary.

Reports Consolidation Act of 2000 (RCA) The Reports Consolidation Act of 2000 (RCA; P.L. 106-531, codified in part at 31 U.S.C. §3516) permits an agency, with OMB concurrence, to package its *Agency Performance Update* (APU, sometimes called an *Annual Performance Report* (APR) or *Program Performance Report* (PPR)) together with certain financial statements and reports. If an agency does so, the consolidated document is referred to as a *Performance and Accountability Report* (PAR). OMB initially required agencies to adopt the PAR format, but now gives

	agencies flexibility to instead submit the APU in February along with the forthcoming year's congressional budget justification and *Agency Performance Plan.*
Strategic Plan (SP)	No longer current law. An agency-level, five-year plan that was required by GPRA 1993 to be updated with a minimum frequency of every three years. GPRAMA replaced these requirements with a substantially different process for developing an *Agency Strategic Plan*, including a requirement for every agency's plan to be updated and aligned with presidential terms instead of providing for staggered updates every three years. GPRAMA's Agency Strategic Plans also have somewhat expanded requirements for their contents, compared to GPRA 1993's version of an agency-level Strategic Plan.
tax expenditures	Defined under current law as revenue losses attributable to provisions of the federal tax laws which allow a special exclusion, exemption, or deduction from gross income or which provide a special credit, a preferential rate of tax, or a deferral of tax liability (P.L. 93-344, as amended (2 U.S.C. §622)). GPRAMA requires discussion of tax expenditures to be included in several products and processes, including *federal government priority goals*, the *Federal Government Performance Plan*, and *OMB quarterly priority progress reviews.*

End Notes

[1] P.L. 111-352, 124 Stat. 3866 (H.R. 2142). The law also has been cited as GPRMA, GPRA 2010, and GPRA.

[2] P.L. 103-62, 107 Stat. 285. Some of GPRA 1993's provisions were amended before enactment of GPRAMA.

[3] GPRA 1993 stood in contrast with past initiatives that several Presidents pursued through their use of discretion. All of the initiatives were generally abandoned due to changes in Administration, a perception of unrealistic ambitions, or lack of congressional buy-in. The initiatives included the Lyndon B. Johnson Administration's Planning-Programming-Budgeting System (PPBS, 1965); the Richard M. Nixon and Gerald R. Ford Administrations' Management by Objectives (MBO, 1973); and the Jimmy Carter Administration's Zero-Base Budgeting (ZBB, 1977). After GPRA1993's enactment, the William Clinton Administration undertook a National Performance Review (NPR, 1993)

and the George W. Bush Administration pursued the President's Management Agenda (PMA, 2001). The Barack Obama Administration has pursued an Accountable Government Initiative (AGI). For discussion of the AGI, see CRS Congressional Distribution Memorandum, *Obama Administration Agenda for Government Performance: Evolution and Related Issues for Congress*, January 19, 2011, by Clinton T. Brass (available on request).

4 U.S. Congress, Senate Committee on Governmental Affairs, *Government Performance and Results Act of 1993*, report to accompany S. 20, 103rd Cong., 1st sess., June 16, 1993, S.Rept. 103-58 (Washington: GPO, 1993), p. 3.

5 For example, as discussed later in this report, agency-level strategic plans under GPRA 1993 were required to cover five years and to be revised every three years. They could be revised at times that suited the circumstances of individual agencies. Under GPRAMA, these products cover four years and are required to be revised and submitted at the same time, every four years, in alignment with the beginning of presidential terms.

6 For discussion, see David H. Rosenbloom, *Building a Legislative-Centered Public Administration: Congress and the Administrative State, 1946-1999* (Tuscaloosa, AL: University of Alabama Press, 2000); and Mathew D. McCubbins and Thomas Schwartz, "Congressional Oversight Overlooked: Police Patrols versus Fire Alarms," *American Journal of Political Science*, vol. 28, no. 1 (February 1984), pp. 165-179.

7 Analysis of the rationales for changing GPRA 1993 and the prospects for GPRAMA to succeed are outside the scope of this report.

8 For committee reports that accompanied the legislation during its development, see U.S. Congress, House Committee on Oversight and Government Reform, *Government Efficiency, Effectiveness, and Performance Improvement Act of 2010*, report to accompany H.R. 2142, 111th Cong., 2nd sess., June 14, 2010, H.Rept. 111-504 (Washington: GPO, 2010); and U.S. Congress, Senate Committee on Homeland Security and Governmental Affairs, *GPRA Modernization Act of 2010*, report to accompany H.R. 2142, 111th Cong., 2nd sess., December 16, 2010, S.Rept. 111-372 (Washington: GPO, 2010). For views about how GPRAMA addressed the findings of Senate Budget Committee's Task Force on Government Performance, see Sen. Mark Warner, remarks in the Senate, *Congressional Record*, daily edition, vol. 156 (September 28, 2010), p. S7630. For discussion of the Obama Administration's performance agenda and some aspects of the George W. Bush Administration performance agenda, see CRS Congressional Distribution Memorandum, *Obama Administration Agenda for Government Performance: Evolution and Related Issues for Congress*, January 19, 2011, by Clinton T. Brass (available on request). GAO suggested that Congress consider changes to GPRA 1993 in U.S. General Accounting Office (later renamed Government Accountability Office, hereafter GAO), *Results-Oriented Government: GPRA Has Established a Solid Foundation for Achieving Greater Results*, GAO-04-38, March 2004.

9 Provisions that GPRAMA did not modify include authority for OMB to exempt agencies with annual outlays of $20 million or less from certain requirements (31 U.S.C. §1117); authority for agencies to receive waivers of non-statutory administrative requirements in order to achieve an ambitious goal (31 U.S.C. §9703); requirements for pilot projects and phased implementation of GPRA 1993 (31 U.S.C. §§1118, 1119, and 9704); a requirement for the Office of Personnel Management to develop a training component on strategic planning and performance measurement for managers (Section 9 of P.L. 103-62; 107 Stat. 295); and separate goal-setting and performance measurement provisions for the U.S. Postal Service (39 U.S.C. §§2801-2805). These provisions are not discussed further in this report.

10 Two other significant provisions do not fit neatly into these categories. One requires the Office of Personnel Management (OPM) to identify skills and competencies needed by government personnel for goal-setting, evaluation, and analysis; incorporate the skills and competencies into relevant position classifications; and work with agencies to incorporate the skills and competencies into employee training (GPRAMA, Section 12; 124 Stat. 3882; 5 U.S.C. §5105 note). Another provision requires GAO to report on the GPRAMA's

implementation (GPRAMA, Section 15; 124 Stat.3883; 31 U.S.C. §1115 note). Specifically, GAO is required to report on the law's early implementation by June 2013.GPRAMA also requires GAO to report on the law's later implementation, with respect to both the CFO Act agencies and executive branch-wide goals and plans, by deadlines in September 2015 and September 2017.

[11] Statutory citations and capsule summaries for individual products, processes, and related terms are provided in Appendix B. Full listings of subcomponents that are required to be included in a product or process may be found in the statutory text. Past experience suggests that when agencies and OMB implement a law like GPRAMA, they may use terms that are different from those specified in law. Generally speaking, this CRS report uses terms as specified in the statutory text. However, the report and Appendix B will be updated to track informal usage.

[12] In Appendix B, see "agency" for discussion of which agencies are covered by GPRAMA.

[13] Under GPRA 1993, agencies were not required to develop Strategic Plans (SPs) according to an identical schedule. The SP covered a future period of at least five fiscal years. The SP was required to be updated with a minimum frequency of every three years, or for the Department of Defense (DOD), every four years. Aside from DOD, an agency could update its plan on a customized schedule.

[14] Apart from the frequency of consultations, the frequency of actual updates to an ASP that Congress may influence could diminish, from a minimum of two out of every three Congresses (under GPRA 1993, two updates every six years, at customized times) to one out of every two Congresses (under GPRAMA, one update every four years, at the beginning of a President's term).

[15] Compared to GPRA 1993, GPRAMA decreases the required frequency of an agency's consultations about its ASP with non-federal stakeholders, from a minimum of once every three years to once every four years. If an ASP is updated once every four years, this type of consultation might occur only at the beginning of a President's term.

[16] Under the Budget and Accounting Act of 1921 (codified at 31 U.S.C. §1108), most executive branch agencies must submit budget requests to the President for potential modification, before the requests are sent to Congress. OMB performs much of this work on the President's behalf. When OMB receives an agency's budget request and Agency Performance Plan, OMB may direct that the products be modified to reflect the President's policy preferences in his or her budget proposal to Congress. Congress later gave authority to some executive agencies to submit budget proposals directly to Congress without modification by the President.

[17] A performance goal is a target level of performance to be achieved in a particular time period; see Appendix B.

[18] GPRAMA provides definitions for terms like these to clarify Congress's meaning; see Appendix B.

[19] In February, when the President's budget proposal is submitted to Congress, four months of the current fiscal year have already passed. There may be changes in goals, targets, or funds for the current fiscal year, compared to the previous APP, that correspond to funding or policy decisions that were made in the interim time period. The requirement to cover the current year may capture such changes.

[20] For ease of reference, this CRS report refers to the product as an Agency Performance Update (APU). Under GPRA 1993, agencies were required to submit an annual Program Performance Report (PPR). OMB later called this product the Annual Performance Report (APR). OMB's use of the non-statutory term "APR" may continue under GPRAMA.

[21] This was the timing requirement for GPRA 1993's equivalent product, the Program Performance Report. As drafted, GPRAMA requires an agency to make the APU available "no less than 150 days" after the end of the fiscal year. This timing requirement would prohibit an agency from making the APU available until 150 days after the end of the fiscal year. This probably is a drafting error. For information about the authors' intent, see U.S.

Congress, Senate Committee on Homeland Security and Governmental Affairs, *GPRA Modernization Act of 2010*, report to accompany H.R. 2142, 111th Cong., 2nd sess., December 16, 2010, S.Rept. 111-372 (Washington: GPO, 2010), p. 16.

[22] The Reports Consolidation Act of 2000 (RCA; P.L. 106-531) permits an agency, with OMB concurrence, to package its Agency Performance Update together with certain financial statements and reports. If an agency does so, the consolidated document is referred to as a Performance and Accountability Report (PAR). OMB requires PARs to be submitted to Congress no later than 45 calendar days after the end of an agency's fiscal year (e.g., November 15), and draft PARs to be submitted to OMB for clearance at least 10 working days before then (see U.S. Executive Office of the President, Office of Management and Budget (hereafter OMB), *Circular No. A-136*, "Financial Reporting Requirements," September 29, 2010, pp. 3-4). OMB initially required all agencies to adopt the PAR format with the earlier, November deadline for the GPRA-required Program Performance Report. Subsequently, OMB gave agencies flexibility to instead submit the Program Performance Report several months later, in February, along with the forthcoming year's congressional budget justification and APP (see ibid., pp. 14-15).

[23] The Chief Financial Officers Act of 1990 (CFO Act; P.L. 101-576) established statutory CFOs in agencies that were listed at 31 U.S.C. §901(b). These twenty-four agencies include the 15 departments and nine other large agencies, and as a group they frequently are called the "CFO Act agencies."

[24] The law says "[e]very 2 years, the head of each agency listed in section 901(b) of [Title 31], *or as otherwise determined by the Director of the Office of Management and Budget*, shall identify agency priority goals from among the performance goals of the agency" (emphasis added; GPRAMA, Section 5; 31 U.S.C. §1120(b)(1)).

[25] CRS Congressional Distribution Memorandum, *Analysis of Subcommittee-Reported H.R. 2142 (111th Congress) and Related Issues*, May 19, 2010, by Clinton T. Brass, p. 7 (available on request). OMB began to convene quarterly reviews of HPPGs in September 2010. Some agencies began conducting their own reviews earlier.

[26] For more details and statutory citations, see "OMB and Agency Reports and Plans on Unmet Goals" in Appendix B.

[27] These requirements expand on a provision from GPRA 1993 that did not specify the plan's contents. Under previous law, GPRA 1993 did not require an agency to submit an Annual Performance Plan (under GPRAMA, Agency Performance Plan) to Congress. Rather, the APP submission was intended to support the President's annual development of a "federal government performance plan." GPRA 1993 did not specify any of the contents of this broader plan. In practice, OMB considered the President's budget proposal to satisfy this statutory requirement. Agencies then submitted their presidentially-modified APPs and budget requests to Congress.

[28] For more information, see Appendix B for the item "OMB performance website." GPRAMA's provision appeared to draw in part from the Obama Administration's plans to establish a performance-related website, Performance.gov. That website was established in 2010 to contain data about HPPGs, but was accessible only in the executive branch. The website was opened to the public in 2011, albeit without HPPG data.

[29] GPRAMA requires agencies to define the term "program" in a way that is consistent with OMB guidance. It might be noted in this context that during the George W. Bush Administration, OMB undertook an initiative to rate all "programs" in the executive branch. From 2003 until the inauguration of President Obama, OMB used the Program Assessment Rating Tool (PART), a questionnaire, to annually assign ratings of "overall effectiveness" to OMB-defined programs. OMB's definitions of "program" for purposes of the PART sometimes were controversial. OMB sometimes aggregated separate programs for the purposes of the PART, while in other cases it disaggregated programs. As a consequence, OMB's PART assessments sometimes were said to correspond to "PART programs," as distinct from how agencies and non-federal stakeholders might define a program. GAO

noted that OMB's aggregation and disaggregation of activities into a PART program sometimes (1) made it difficult to select performance measures for PART programs that had multiple missions, or (2) ignored the context in which programs operated. See GAO, *Performance Budgeting: Observations on the Use of OMB's Program Assessment Rating Tool for the Fiscal Year 2004 Budget*, GAO-04-174, January 2004, pp. 29-30.

[30] Specifically, it remains to be seen whether OMB will interpret a general frequency-of-update requirement as applying to data items that do not explicitly call for quarterly information. In 31 U.S.C. §1122, GPRAMA requires OMB to operate the website. In this context, the only explicit mentions of quarterly information are two requirements to provide "results achieved during the most recent quarter" for agency priority goals and federal government priority goals. It remains to be seen if other information about priority goals will be updated quarterly. Other provisions require products or information to be posted on the OMB performance website but are silent with regard to frequency or seem to contemplate other frequencies of updating. For example, GPRAMA requires data from the Federal Government Performance Plan to be included on the website and updated annually. In addition, Agency Strategic Plans, Agency Performance Plans, and Agency Performance Updates are required to be posted on the website, but these products reflect snapshots in time according to their schedules for publication and may not be updated quarterly.

[31] Presidents may attempt to treat as non-binding a statutory provision that says the President or OMB "may" or "shall" make legislative recommendations. Presidential signing statements sometimes justify this view by using language from Article II, Section 3 of the Constitution, which says the President "shall ... recommend to [Congress's] Consideration such Measures as he shall judge necessary and expedient." For example, see U.S. National Archives and Records Administration, *George W. Bush White House Web Site*, "Statement by the President," November 25, 2002, at http://georgewbush-whitehouse.archives.gov/news/releases/2002/11/20021125-11.html.

[32] For the agency-level requirement, see the earlier heading "Lists of plans and reports produced for Congress."

[33] The statutory PIO position focuses on several activities, including goal-setting, planning, management, measurement, analysis, and employee performance appraisal. The duties are similar to those that were included in Executive Order (E.O.) 13450, which the George W. Bush Administration used to establish the position in 2007. However, the extent to which these varied activities may fit effectively into the competencies of one position remains to be seen. PIOs have operated with little transparency since the beginning of their activities in January 2008. Nevertheless, a pre-GPRAMA study of PIOs found several challenges to their effectiveness. These included "that [PIOs] often have multiple duties that include budget and financial issues, causing them to give performance management short shrift" (see Partnership for Public Service and Grant Thornton, *A Critical Role at a Critical Time: A Survey of Performance Improvement Officers*, April 2011, p. 1). Along these lines, GPRAMA does not require a PIO to have performance-related duties as his or her primary duty. In addition, observers have noted that government performance policy has had two distinct orientations: (1) goal-setting and performance measurement and (2) program evaluation. GPRA 1993 especially focused on the former. This tendency led the evaluation community to argue for elevating the salience of program evaluation in federal officials and organizations. See American Evaluation Association, *An Evaluation Roadmap for a More Effective Government*, September 2010, pp. 8-10, at http://www.eval.org/EPTF/aea10.roadmap.101910.pdf.

[34] In 2009, the Senate Committee on Appropriations directed OMB to include a budget justification for the PIC in the annual budget request for the Executive Office of the President (EOP) beginning with the President's FY2011 budget proposal. Subsequently, the EOP budget request has provided some information about the PIC's activities and plans. For the committee's directive, see U.S. Congress, Senate Committee on Appropriations, *Financial Services and General Government Appropriations Bill*, 2010, report to

accompany S. 1432, 111th Cong., 1st sess., July 9, 2009,S.Rept. 111-43 (Washington: GPO, 2009), p. 40.

[35] Section 9 of GPRAMA (31 U.S.C. §1124(b)(3)) says that heads of agencies whose PIOs serve on the PIC "shall, as appropriate and to the extent permitted by law, provide at the request of the chairperson of the [PIC] up to 2 personnel authorizations to serve at the direction of the chairperson." GPRAMA identifies the DDM as the PIC's chairperson.

[36] An Agency Performance Update is required to cover the same time period as the relevant Agency Performance Plan. The precise years that are covered, however, may depend on whether an agency chooses to package the APU along with the agency budget request or with an agency's Performance and Accountability Report. On one hand, budget requests are due to Congress in February, several months after the beginning of a fiscal year. PARs are due in November, just after the end of a fiscal year. If an agency submits its APU in February 2014 along with the FY2015 budget request, the APU would be required to cover all of FY2013 and the first few months of FY2014, the same time period as the previously submitted Agency Performance Plan (FY2013-FY2014). If an agency submits its APU in November 2013 along with its PAR, by contrast, it remains to be seen whether the APU would cover only FY2013 and omit FY2014 (because little time would have passed in FY2014) or cover the same time period as the earlier APP (the two fiscal years FY2012 and FY2013). In either case, FY2013 would appear to be included.

[37] American Evaluation Association, *An Evaluation Roadmap for a More Effective Government*, September 2010, pp. 8-9, at http://www.eval.org/EPTF/aea10.roadmap.101910.pdf. In practice, however, it may be noted that evaluation and measurement often are complementary. Performance measurement might be characterized as answering the question "where are we?", and evaluation may answer questions such as "what influences did a program have?", "how and why?", and "what might be done to improve?" Measures and evaluation may be integrated through a logic model (see Appendix B), which shows how activities in one or more programs align with results (or more specifically, how disparate inputs, activities, and outputs are expected to influence one or more desired policy outcomes).

[38] OMB's website lists (1) budget development and execution and (2) management as two of these five processes. The website also says that the budgeting role is "a mechanism by which a President implements decisions, policies, priorities, and actions in all areas (from economic recovery to health care to energy policy to national security)." OMB, "The Mission and Structure of the Office of Management and Budget," at http://www.whitehouse.gov/omb/ organization_mission/.

[39] These include the possibilities of OMB selecting priority goals; populating the performance-related website; directing agencies to provide staff to support the OMB-directed PIC; deciding when an agency's performance goal is considered to be "unmet"; guiding agencies on how to define the term "program"; and, via OMB's role in developing the President's budget proposal, influencing or directing how agencies identify any "low priority program activities" and "outdated or duplicative" reports to Congress.

[40] See, for example, OMB's direction to agencies on revisions to strategic plans during the transition from GPRA 1993 to GPRAMA (OMB, *Circular No. A-11*, Section 210, "Preparing and Submitting an Agency Strategic Plan," August 2011, pp. 4-5).

[41] GPRAMA also decreases the statutorily required frequency of an agency's consultations about its Agency Strategic Plan with non-federal stakeholders. As a result, this type of consultation might occur only in the first year of a President's term. It remains to be seen whether this change may affect the ability of non-federal stakeholders to influence agencies' choices.

[42] Under GPRA 1993, nearly all of the law's duties to produce plans and reports were vested with agency heads rather than OMB. Following enactment of GPRA 1993, OMB was quick to require that agencies submit documents to OMB for review and clearance—that is, potential modification before release in order to conform to presidential policy views. When an

agency developed a Strategic Plan, for example, OMB required the agency to submit the plan to OMB for clearance at least 45 days prior to submission to Congress (see OMB, *Circular No. A-11*, Part 2, "Preparation and Submission of Strategic Plans," June 1996, p. 237). However, whenever agencies produced such documents, they typically chose when to make a revision and "moved first" in completing full versions of these documents, without direct or sustained OMB involvement in their initial preparation. In other words, OMB's influence on such documents likely most often focused on an end-of-the-process clearance and modification role, as opposed to full-process direction or participation.

[43] It may be difficult or burdensome for an observer to track changes to a website's contents if information is presented in formats other than discrete files (e.g., PDF). Nevertheless, information about changes to a website's contents might be captured if the website provides a bulk-download capability through which an observer could take a "snapshot" in time of the website's contents. This kind of issue may become more salient when information is provided primarily or only on the Internet in machine-readable format. As noted earlier, the OMB performance website is required to present its contents in machine-readable format.

[44] For discussion of the potential for implementation of performance initiatives to create perverse incentives, see CRS Congressional Distribution Memorandum, *Obama Administration Agenda for Government Performance: Evolution and Related Issues for Congress*, January 19, 2011, by Clinton T. Brass (available on request).

[45] P.L. 111-139, Title II (124 Stat. 29). GAO's first report that was issued in compliance with this requirement was released in March 2011. See Section I of U.S. Government Accountability Office, *Opportunities to Reduce Potential Duplication in Government Programs, Save Tax Dollars, and Enhance Revenue*, GAO-11-318SP, March 2011, pp. 1-154.

[46] For example, see U.S. Government Accountability Office, *A Glossary of Terms Used in the Federal Budget Process*, GAO-05-734SP, September 2005; and CRS Report 98-721, *Introduction to the Federal Budget Process*, coordinated by Bill Heniff Jr. Similar publications are available for other government processes like rulemaking and procurement, where Congress also has legislated in detail and, in varying degrees, has involved itself in administration of policy.

[47] Some terms may have specific meanings in fields such as policy analysis, performance measurement, program evaluation, management, and budgeting.

[48] As noted in this report, implementation of GPRAMA will result in presentation of many plans and reports to Congress for scrutiny and potential use. The law also requires most of the products to be made available to the public, which may assist Congress in its legislative work.

[49] Full listings of the subcomponents of various products and processes may be found in the statutory text (124 Stat. 3866). As a convention, some terms in this CRS report and glossary are capitalized. Where relevant, the glossary shows acronyms that are used in this CRS report. A separate table containing acronyms is included as Appendix A. Past experience suggests that when agencies and OMB implement a law like GPRAMA, they may use terms and acronyms that are different from those specified in law. Updates to this report will note significant developments in this regard.

[50] GPRAMA requires an agency to make the APU available "no less than 150 days" after the end of the fiscal year. As drafted, the timing requirement would prohibit an agency from making the APU available until 150 days after the end of the fiscal year. This probably is a drafting error. For information about the authors' intent, see U.S. Congress, Senate Committee on Homeland Security and Governmental Affairs, *GPRA Modernization Act of 2010*, report to accompany H.R. 2142, 111th Cong., 2nd sess., December 16, 2010, S.Rept. 111-372 (Washington: GPO, 2010), p. 16.

[51] OMB, *Circular No. A-11*, Section 230, "Preparing and Submitting an Annual Performance Report," August 2011, p. 2.

[52] The Chief Financial Officers Act of 1990 (CFO Act; 104 Stat. 2838; now codified in Title 31 of the *U.S. Code*) established statutory CFOs in agencies that were listed at 31 U.S.C.

§901(b). These twenty-four agencies are among the largest in the executive branch and frequently are called the "CFO Act agencies."

[53] For discussion, see CRS Congressional Distribution Memorandum, *Obama Administration Agenda for Government Performance: Evolution and Related Issues for Congress*, January 19, 2011, by Clinton T. Brass, pp. 33-35 (available on request), and CRS Report RL33301, *Congress and Program Evaluation: An Overview of Randomized Controlled Trials (RCTs) and Related Issues*, by Clinton T. Brass, Erin D. Williams, and Blas Nuñez-Neto.

[54] U.S. Congress, Senate Committee on Homeland Security and Governmental Affairs, *GPRA Modernization Act of 2010*, report to accompany H.R. 2142, 111th Cong., 2nd sess., December 16, 2010, S.Rept. 111-372 (Washington: GPO, 2010), p. 8.

[55] In a job training program, for example, an agency may offer classes to clients. The classes might be considered to be an activity. The classes culminate with clients who complete a course. These course completions might be called an output. If the clients learn new skills—an intermediate outcome—they may have a better chance of finding employment or increasing earnings, which might be viewed as end outcomes. A logic model also may show how multiple activities in an agency or across agencies align with one or more goals.

[56] Program evaluations, performance measurements, and logic models typically complement each other when they inform policy making, oversight, or study. Like other kinds of policy analysis, these tools may raise more refined questions about how well a program is working or the circumstances that may be necessary for achieving success.

[57] The so-called CFO Act agencies were identified in the Chief Financial Officers Act of 1990 (P.L. 101-576), and the list is codified at 31 U.S.C. §901(b).

[58] E.O. 13450, "Improving Government Program Performance," 72 *Federal Register* 64519, November 13, 2007. The E.O. appeared to formally centralize in OMB some decision making about how agencies implement GPRA 1993. A Bush Administration OMB official was quoted to say the E.O. was issued as "an effort to sustain what we think is valuable beyond this administration" (Robert Brodsky, "Commanding Performance," *National Journal*, April 19, 2008, p. 65).

[59] Some executive agencies are allowed to submit budget proposals directly to Congress without modification, and budget proposals for the legislative and judicial branches are included without change.

In: Modernization of the Government … ISBN: 978-1-62257-383-7
Editors: R. Hawkins and T. P. Duncan

Chapter 2

MANAGING FOR RESULTS: GPRA MODERNIZATION ACT IMPLEMENTATION PROVIDES IMPORTANT OPPORTUNITIES TO ADDRESS GOVERNMENT CHALLENGES*

STATEMENT OF GENE L. DODARO
COMPTROLLER GENERAL OF THE UNITED STATES

United States Government Accountability Office

WHY GAO DID THIS STUDY

The federal government is the world's largest and most complex entity, with about $3.5 trillion in outlays in fiscal year 2010 that fund a broad array of programs and operations. GAO's long-term simulations of the federal budget show—absent policy change—growing deficits accumulating to an unsustainable increase in debt. While the spending side is driven by rising health care costs and demographics, other areas should also be scrutinized. In addition, there are significant performance and management challenges that the federal government needs to confront.

* This is an edited, reformatted and augmented version of United States Government Accountability Office publication, GAO-11-617T, dated May 10, 2011.

GAO was asked to testify on the Government Performance and Results Act (GPRA) Modernization Act of 2010 (GPRAMA), as the administration begins implementing the act. This statement is based on GAO's past and ongoing work on GPRA implementation, as well as recently issued reports (1) identifying opportunities to reduce potential duplication in government programs, save tax dollars, and enhance revenue; and (2) updating GAO's list of government operations at high risk due to their greater vulnerabilities to fraud, waste, abuse, and mismanagement, or the need for transformation. As required by GPRAMA, GAO will periodically evaluate implementation of the act and report to Congress on its findings and recommendations.

WHAT GAO FOUND

GAO's past and ongoing work illustrates how GPRAMA could, if effectively implemented, help address government challenges in five areas:

Instituting a more coordinated and crosscutting approach to achieving meaningful results. GPRAMA could help inform reexamination or restructuring efforts and lead to more effective, efficient, and economical service delivery in overlapping program areas by identifying the various agencies and federal activities—including spending programs, regulations, and tax expenditures—that contribute to crosscutting outcomes. These program areas could include numerous teacher quality initiatives or multiple employment and training programs, among others.

Focusing on addressing weaknesses in major management functions. Agencies need more effective management capabilities to better implement their programs and policies. GPRAMA requires long-term goals to improve management functions in five key areas: financial, human capital, information technology, procurement and acquisition, and real property management. GAO's work has highlighted opportunities for improvements in each of these areas and aspects of all of them are on the GAO high risk list.

Ensuring performance information is both useful and used in decision making. Agencies need to consider the differing needs of various stakeholders, including Congress, to ensure that performance information will be both useful and used. For performance information to be useful, it must be complete, accurate, valid, timely, and easy to use. Yet decision makers often do not have the quality performance information they need to improve results. To help address this need, GPRAMA requires (1) disclosure of information about accuracy and validity, (2) data on crosscutting areas, and (3) quarterly reporting on priority goals on a publicly available Web site.

Sustaining leadership commitment and accountability for achieving results. Perhaps the single most important element of successful management improvement initiatives is the demonstrated commitment of top leaders, as shown by their personal involvement in reform efforts. GPRAMA assigns responsibilities to a Chief Operating Officer and Performance Improvement Officer in each agency to improve agency management and performance.

Engaging Congress in identifying management and performance issues to address. In order for performance improvement initiatives to be useful to Congress for its decision making, garnering congressional buy-in on what to measure and how to present this information is critical. GAO has previously noted the importance of considering Congress a partner in shaping agency goals at the outset. GPRAMA significantly enhances requirements for agencies to consult with Congress.

Chairmen Akaka and Carper, Ranking Members Johnson and Brown, and Members of the Subcommittees:

Thank you for the opportunity to discuss the Government Performance and Results Act (GPRA) Modernization Act of 2010 (GPRAMA)[1] as the administration begins implementing the act. If effectively implemented, the act offers many important opportunities to focus attention on successfully improving the effectiveness of government programs and operations, and addressing significant fiscal, performance, and management challenges facing the federal government.[2] The federal government is the world's largest and most complex entity, with about $3.5 trillion in outlays in fiscal year 2010 that fund a broad array of programs and operations. Looking forward, our long-term simulations of the government's financial condition underscore the need to begin addressing the long-term federal fiscal outlook. Absent changes in fiscal policy, the structural imbalance between spending and revenue paths lead to large and growing deficits. The accumulation of large deficits leads to an unsustainable increase in debt over the long term.[3] This, in turn, will limit budget flexibility and the federal government's ability to respond to future challenges.

Addressing these fiscal challenges will require action on several fronts. First, all federal programs and activities—discretionary programs, mandatory spending, revenues, and tax expenditures—need to be reexamined. Second, program structures that are outmoded, overlapping, duplicative, fragmented, and not up to the challenges of the times must be reformed or restructured. In this regard, we recently issued a report that identified over 80 areas of potential duplication, overlap, or fragmentation as well as cost savings and revenue-enhancing opportunities.[4] In addition, weaknesses in management capacity, both governmentwide and in individual agencies, undermine efficient and effective government. Here too, our recent update to our high-risk list identified numerous opportunities to reduce costs and improve government performance.[5]

Moving forward, GPRAMA can offer important opportunities to help make tough choices in setting priorities as well as reforming programs and management practices to better link resources to results. The various provisions of the act are to be implemented over the next few years. Most of the enhanced planning and reporting requirements at both the governmentwide and agency levels are to be implemented in 2012 and beyond (see appendix I for a more detailed implementation schedule). Thus far, the administration has tasked each agency to assign top leadership responsibility for leading their management and performance improvement efforts, including quarterly reviews of performance, which are to begin no later than this June. Sustained and visible top leadership support will be critical to ensuring successful implementation of the act's provisions.

My statement today, which is based on our past and ongoing work, will focus on five key areas where implementing GPRAMA could help address government challenges. In particular, the act calls for:

- instituting a more coordinated and crosscutting approach to achieving meaningful results,
- focusing on addressing weaknesses in major management functions,
- ensuring performance information is both useful and used in decision making,
- sustaining leadership commitment and accountability for achieving results, and
- engaging Congress in identifying management and performance issues to address.

Finally, my statement will speak to GAO's role in evaluating implementation of this act.

Instituting a More Coordinated and Crosscutting Approach to Achieving Meaningful Results

The federal government faces a series of challenges that in many instances are not possible for any single agency to address alone. Many federal program efforts, including those related to ensuring food safety, providing homeland security, monitoring incidence of infectious diseases, or improving response to natural disasters, transcend more than one agency. Agencies face a range of challenges and barriers when they attempt to work collaboratively. GPRAMA establishes a new framework aimed at taking a more crosscutting and integrated approach to focusing on results and improving government performance. It requires the Office of Management and Budget (OMB), in coordination with agencies, to develop—every 4 years—long-term, outcome-oriented goals for a limited number of crosscutting policy areas. On an annual basis, OMB is to provide information on how these long-term crosscutting goals will be achieved.

Also, we recently reported that a system of key national indicators currently under development in the U.S.[6] could contribute to the implementation of the act's requirements for establishing crosscutting goals as well as agency-level goals.[7] Such a system aims to aggregate essential statistical measures of economic, social, and environmental issues to provide reliable information on a country's condition, offering a shared frame of reference that enables collective accountability. Federal officials could look to measures included in a system of key national indicators to highlight areas in need of improvement and could use this information to inform the selection of future crosscutting and agency-level goals. Also, by providing information on economic, social, and environmental conditions and trends across the nation, a key indicator system may help provide context and a broader perspective for interpreting how the federal government's efforts contribute to national outcomes.

The crosscutting approach required by the act will provide a much needed basis for more fully integrating a wide array of federal activities as well as a cohesive perspective on the long-term goals of the federal government that is focused on priority policy areas. It could also be a valuable tool for governmentwide reexamination of existing programs and for considering proposals for new programs.

Our recent report on duplication, overlap, and fragmentation highlights a number of areas where a more crosscutting approach is needed—both across agencies and within a specific agency. We found that duplication and overlap occur because programs have been added incrementally over time to respond to new needs and challenges, without a strategy to minimize duplication, overlap, and fragmentation among them. Also, there are not always interagency mechanisms or strategies in place to coordinate programs that address crosscutting issues, which can lead to potentially duplicative, overlapping, and fragmented efforts.

Effective GPRAMA implementation could help inform reexamination or restructuring efforts related to these and other areas by identifying the various agencies and federal activities—including spending programs, regulations, and tax expenditures—that contribute to each crosscutting goal. These efforts could also be supported by a system of key national indicators. For example, to influence positive movement in certain indicators, federal officials could look at all the programs that contribute to improving outcomes related to those indicators, examine how each contributes, and use this information to streamline and align the programs to create a more effective and efficient approach.

Examples from our work on duplication, overlap, and fragmentation include:

- Teacher quality programs: In fiscal year 2009, the federal government spent over $4 billion specifically to improve the quality of our nation's 3 million teachers through numerous programs across the government.8 Federal efforts to improve teacher quality have led to the creation and expansion of a variety of programs across the federal government; however, there is no governmentwide strategy to minimize fragmentation, overlap, or duplication among these many programs. Specifically, we identified 82 distinct programs designed to help improve teacher quality, either as a primary purpose or as an allowable activity, administered across 10 federal agencies. The proliferation of programs has resulted in fragmentation that can frustrate agency efforts to administer programs in a comprehensive manner, limit the ability to determine which programs are most cost effective, and ultimately increase program costs.

  Department of Education (Education) officials believe that federal programs have failed to make significant progress in helping states close achievement gaps between schools serving students from different socioeconomic backgrounds, because in part, federal programs that focus on teaching and learning of specific subjects are too fragmented to help state and district officials strengthen instruction and increase student achievement in a comprehensive manner. Education has established working groups to help develop more effective collaboration across Education offices, and has reached out to other agencies to develop a framework for sharing information on some teacher quality activities, but it has noted that coordination efforts do not always prove useful and cannot fully eliminate barriers to program alignment.

Congress could help eliminate some of these barriers through legislation, particularly through the pending reauthorization of the Elementary and Secondary Education Act of 1965 and other key education bills. Specifically, to minimize any wasteful fragmentation and overlap among teacher quality programs, Congress may choose either to eliminate programs that are too small to evaluate cost effectively or to combine programs serving similar target groups into a larger program. Education has already proposed combining 38 programs into 11 programs in its reauthorization proposal, which could allow the agency to dedicate a higher portion of its administrative resources to monitoring programs for results and providing technical assistance.

- *Military health system:* The Department of Defense's (DOD) Military Health System (MHS) costs have more than doubled from $19 billion in fiscal year 2001 to $49 billion in 2010 and are expected to increase to over $62 billion by 2015. The responsibilities and authorities for the MHS are distributed among several organizations within DOD with no central command authority or single entity accountable for minimizing costs and achieving efficiencies. Under the MHS's current command structure, the Office of the Assistant Secretary of Defense for Health Affairs, the Army, the Navy, and the Air Force each has its own headquarters and associated support functions.

  DOD has taken limited actions to date to consolidate certain common administrative, management, and clinical functions within its MHS. To reduce duplication in its command structure and eliminate redundant processes that add to growing defense health care costs, DOD could take action to further assess alternatives for restructuring the governance structure of the military health system. In 2006, if

DOD and the services had chosen to implement one of the reorganization alternatives studied by a DOD working group, a May 2006 report by the Center for Naval Analyses showed that DOD could have achieved significant savings. Our adjustment of those savings from 2005 into 2010 dollars indicates those savings could range from $281 million to $460 million annually, depending on the alternative chosen and the numbers of military, civilian, and contractor positions eliminated. The Under Secretary of Defense for Personnel and Readiness has recently established a new position to oversee DOD's military healthcare reform efforts.

- *Employment and training programs:* In fiscal year 2009, 47 federal employment and training programs in nine agencies spent about $18 billion to provide services, such as job search and job counseling, to program participants.[9] Most of these programs are administered by the Departments of Labor, Education, and Health and Human Services (HHS). Forty-four of the 47 programs we identified, including those with broader missions such as multipurpose block grants, overlap with at least one other program in that they provide at least one similar service to a similar population. As we reported in January 2011, nearly all 47 programs track multiple outcome measures, but only five programs have had an impact study completed since 2004 to assess whether outcomes resulted from the program and not some other cause. We examined potential duplication among three selected large programs—HHS's Temporary Assistance for Needy Families (TANF) and the Department of Labor's Employment Service, and Workforce Investment Act of 1998 (WIA) Adult programs—and found they provide some of the same services to the same population through separate administrative structures.

  Colocating services and consolidating administrative structures may increase efficiencies and reduce costs, but implementation can be challenging. Some states have colocated TANF employment and training services in one-stop centers where Employment Service and WIA Adult services are provided. An obstacle to further progress in achieving greater administrative efficiencies is that little information is available about the strategies and results of such initiatives. In addition, little is known about the incentives that states and localities have to undertake such initiatives and whether additional incentives are needed.

To facilitate further progress by states and localities in increasing administrative efficiencies in employment and training programs, we recommended in 2011 that the Secretaries of Labor and HHS work together to develop and disseminate information that could inform such efforts. As part of this effort, Labor and HHS should examine the incentives for states and localities to undertake such initiatives and, as warranted, identify options for increasing such incentives. Labor and HHS agreed they should develop and disseminate this information. HHS noted that it does not have the legal authority to mandate increased TANF-WIA coordination or create incentives for such efforts. As part of its proposed changes to the Workforce Investment Act of 1998, the administration proposes consolidating nine programs into three. In addition, the budget proposal would transfer the Senior Community Service Employment Program from Labor to HHS. Sustained oversight by Congress could also help ensure progress is realized.

Focusing on Addressing Weaknesses in Major Management Functions

Although agencies have made progress improving their operations in recent years, they need more effective management capabilities to better implement new programs and policies. As part of the new governmentwide framework created by GPRAMA, OMB is required to develop long-term goals to improve management functions across the government. The act specifies that these goals should include five areas: financial management, human capital management, information technology management, procurement and acquisition management, and real property management.[10] All five of these areas have been identified by GAO as key management challenges across the government.[11]

Moreover, some aspects of these areas have warranted our designation as high risk, either governmentwide or at certain agencies. For example, although significant improvements have been made since we initially designated it as high risk in 2001, strategic human capital management in the federal government remains high risk because of a need to address current and emerging critical skills gaps that are undermining agencies' abilities to meet their vital missions. Another example is financial management at DOD, which we designated as high risk in 1995 due to pervasive financial and related business management systems and control deficiencies.

In addition, a number of the cost-savings or revenue-enhancement opportunities we recently identified touch on needed improvements to management functions.[12] Examples include:

- *Noncompetitive contracts:* Federal agencies generally are required to award contracts competitively, but a substantial amount of federal money is being obligated on noncompetitive contracts annually. Federal agencies obligated approximately $170 billion on noncompetitive contracts in fiscal year 2009 alone. While there has been some fluctuation over the years, the percentage of obligations under noncompetitive contracts recently has been in the range of 31 percent to over 35 percent.

  Although some agency decisions to forego competition may be justified, we found that when federal agencies decide to open their contracts to competition, they frequently realize savings. For example, the Department of State (State) awarded a noncompetitive contract for installation and maintenance of technical security equipment at U.S. embassies in 2003. In response to our recommendation, State subsequently competed this requirement, and in 2007 it awarded contracts to four small businesses for a total savings of over $218 million. In another case, we found in 2006 that the Army had awarded noncompetitive contracts for security guards, but later spent 25 percent less for the same services when the contracts were competed.

  In July 2009, OMB called for agencies to reduce obligations under new contract actions that are awarded using high-risk contracting authorities by 10 percent in fiscal year 2010. These high-risk contracts include those that are awarded noncompetitively and those that are structured as competitive but for which only one offer is received. While sufficient data are not yet available to determine whether OMB's goal was met, we are currently reviewing the agencies' savings plans to identify steps taken toward that goal, and will continue to monitor the progress agencies make toward achieving this and any subsequent goals set by OMB.
- *Undisbursed grant balances:* Past audits of federal agencies by GAO and Inspectors General, as well as agencies' annual performance reports, have suggested grant management challenges, including

failure to conduct grant closeouts and undisbursed balances, are a long-standing problem. In August 2008, we reported that during calendar year 2006, about $1 billion in undisbursed funding remained in expired grant accounts in HHS's Payment Management System—the largest civilian grant payment system, which multiple agencies use. In August 2008, we recommended that OMB instruct all executive departments and independent agencies to track undisbursed balances in expired grant accounts and report on the resolution of this funding in their annual performance plan and Performance and Accountability Reports. As of April 2011, OMB had not issued guidance to all agencies to track and report on such balances.

- *Unneeded real property:* Many federal agencies hold real property they do not need, including property that is excess or underutilized. Excess and underutilized properties present significant potential risks to federal agencies because they are costly to maintain. For example, in fiscal year 2009, agencies reported underutilized buildings accounted for over $1.6 billion in annual operating costs. In a June 2010 Presidential Memorandum to federal agencies, the administration established a new target of saving $3 billion through disposals and other methods by the end of fiscal year 2012; the President reiterated this goal in his 2012 budget. However, federal agencies continue to face obstacles to disposing of unneeded property, such as requirements to offer the property to other federal agencies, then to state and local governments and certain nonprofits at no cost. If these entities cannot use the property, agencies may also need to comply with costly historic preservation or environmental cleanup requirements before disposing of the property. Finally, community stakeholders may oppose agencies' plans for property disposal.

OMB could assist agencies in meeting their property disposal target by implementing our April 2007 recommendation of developing an action plan to address key problems associated with disposing of unneeded real property, including reducing the effect of competing stakeholder interests on real property decisions. The President's fiscal year 2012 budget proposed the Civilian Property Realignment Act (CPRA), which was recently introduced in the House of Representatives. The act would establish a Civilian Property Realignment Board modeled on the Base Closure and Realignment Commission. We are engaged in discussions with Congress to determine how we can best support Congress, should the act become law.

ENSURING PERFORMANCE INFORMATION IS BOTH USEFUL AND USED IN DECISION MAKING

Agencies need to consider the differing information needs of various users—such as agency top leadership and line managers, OMB, and Congress—to ensure that performance information will be both useful and used in decision making. We have previously reported that to be useful, performance information must meet diverse users' needs for completeness, accuracy, validity, timeliness, and ease of use. GPRAMA puts into place several requirements that could address these needs.

- *Completeness:* Agencies often lack information on the effectiveness of programs; such information could help decision makers prioritize resources among programs. Our work on overlap and duplication has found crosscutting areas where performance information is limited or does not exist. For example, not enough is known about the effectiveness of many domestic food assistance programs—an area where three federal agencies administer 18 programs, covering more than $62.5 billion in spending in fiscal year 2008. Research suggests that participation in 7 of the 18 programs—including the Special Supplemental Nutrition Program for Women, Infants, and Children (WIC), the National School Lunch Program, the School Breakfast Program, and SNAP—is associated with positive health and nutrition outcomes consistent with programs' goals, such as raising the level of nutrition among low-income households, safeguarding the health and well-being of the nation's children, and strengthening the agricultural economy. Yet little is known about the effectiveness of the remaining 11 programs because they have not been well studied. In another area, economic development, where four agencies administer 80 programs, a lack of information on program outcomes is a current and long-standing problem. In shedding light on these and other areas, the newcrosscutting planning and reporting requirements could lead to the development of performance information in areas that are currently incomplete.

- *Accuracy and validity:* Agencies are required to disclose more information about the accuracy and validity of their performance information in their performance plans and reports, including the sources for their data and actions to address limitations to the data.
- *Timeliness and ease of use:* While agencies will continue to report annually on progress towards the rest of their goals, GPRAMA requires reporting for governmentwide and agency priority goals on a quarterly basis. By also requiring information to be posted on a governmentwide Web site, the act will make performance information more accessible and easy to use by stakeholders and the public, thus fostering transparency and civic engagement.

In addition, to help ensure that performance information is used—not simply collected and reported as a compliance exercise—GPRAMA requires top leadership and program officials to be involved in quarterly reviews of priority goals. During these sessions, they are expected to review the progress achieved toward goals; assess the contributions of underlying federal organizations, programs, and activities; categorize goals by their risk of not being achieved; and develop strategies to improve performance.

To be successful, these officials must have the knowledge and experience necessary to use and trust the information they are gathering. Building analytical capacity to use performance information and to ensure its quality—both in terms of staff trained to do the analysis and availability of research and evaluation resources—is critical to using performance information in a meaningful fashion and will play a large role in the success of government performance improvements. Federal officials must understand how the performance information they gather can be used to provide insight into the factors that impede or contribute to program successes; assess the effect of the program; or help explain the linkages between program inputs, activities, outputs, and outcomes.

Our periodic surveys of federal managers on government performance and management issues have found a positive relationship between agencies providing training and development on setting program performance goals and the use of performance information when setting or revising performance goals.[13] These surveys have also found a significant increase in training between our initial survey in 1997 and our most recent one in 2007.[14] However, only about half of our survey respondents in 2007 reported receiving any training that would assist in strategic planning and performance assessment. We previously recommended that OMB ensure that agencies are making adequate investments in training on performance planning and measurement, with a particular emphasis on how to use performance information to improve program performance.[15] Consistent with this, according to the President's Fiscal Year 2012 Budget, in the coming year OMB and the Performance Improvement Council intend to help agencies strengthen their employees' skills in analyzing and using performance information to achieve greater results.[16]

To further develop this capacity, within 1 year of enactment, GPRAMA requires the Office of Personnel Management (OPM), in consultation with the Performance Improvement Council, to identify the key skills and competencies needed by federal employees to carry out a variety of performance management activities including developing goals, evaluating programs, and analyzing and using performance information. Once those key skills and competencies are identified, OPM is then required to incorporate those skills and competencies into relevant position classifications and agency training no later than 2 years after enactment.

SUSTAINING LEADERSHIP COMMITMENT AND ACCOUNTABILITY FOR ACHIEVING RESULTS

Perhaps the single most important element of successful management improvement initiatives is the demonstrated commitment of top leaders. This commitment is most prominently shown through the personal involvement of top leaders in developing and directing reform efforts. Organizations that successfully address their long-standing management weaknesses do not "staff out" responsibility for leading change. Top leadership involvement and clear lines of accountability for making management improvements are critical to overcoming organizations' natural resistance to change, marshalling the resources needed in many cases to improve management, and building and maintaining the organizationwide commitment to new ways of doing business.

GPRAMA creates several new leadership structures and responsibilities aimed at sustaining attention on improvement efforts at both the agency and governmentwide levels. The act designates the deputy head of each agency as Chief Operating Officer (COO), with overall responsibilities for improving the management and performance of the agency. In addition, the act requires each agency to designate a senior executive as Performance Improvement Officer (PIO) to support the COO. The act also establishes a Performance

Improvement Council—chaired by the OMB Deputy Director for Management and composed of PIOs from various agencies—to assist the Director of OMB in carrying out the governmentwide planning and reporting requirements.

GPRAMA also creates individual and organizational accountability provisions that have the potential to keep attention focused on achieving results. For each governmentwide performance goal, a lead government official is to be designated and held responsible for coordinating efforts to achieve the goal. Similarly, at the agency level, for each performance goal, an agency official, known as a goal leader, will be responsible for achieving the goal. To promote overall organizational accountability, the act requires OMB to report each year on unmet agency goals. Where a goal has been unmet for 3 years, OMB can identify the program for termination or restructuring, among other actions.

ENGAGING CONGRESS IN IDENTIFYING MANAGEMENT AND PERFORMANCE ISSUES TO ADDRESS

In order for performance improvement initiatives to be useful to Congress for its decision making, garnering congressional buy-in on what to measure and how to present this information is critical. In past reviews, we have noted the importance of considering Congress a partner in shaping agency goals at the outset. Congressional committee staff, in discussing the Program Assessment Review Tool (PART)[17] developed by the previous administration, told us that communicating the PART assessment results was not a replacement for the benefit of early consultation between Congress and OMB about what they consider to be the most important performance issues and program areas warranting review.[18]

While GPRA called for agencies to consult with Congress on their strategic plans, the act did not provide detailed or specific requirements on the consultation process or how agencies were to treat information obtained. GPRAMA significantly enhances requirements for agencies to consult with Congress when establishing or adjusting governmentwide and agency goals. OMB and agencies are to consult with relevant committees, obtaining majority and minority views, about proposed goals at least once every 2 years. In addition, OMB and agencies are to describe on the governmentwide Web site or in their strategic plans, respectively, how they incorporated congressional input into their goals.

Beyond this opportunity to provide input to OMB and agencies as they shape their plans, Congress can also play a decisive role in fostering results-oriented cultures in the federal government by using information on agency goals and results as it carries out its legislative responsibilities. For example, authorizing, appropriations, and oversight committees could schedule hearings to determine if agency programs have clear performance goals, measures, and data with which to track progress and whether the programs are achieving their goals. Where goals and objectives are unclear or not results oriented, Congress could articulate the program outcomes it expects agencies to achieve. This would provide important guidance to agencies that could then be incorporated in agency strategic and annual performance plans. Most important, congressional use of agency goals and measured results in its decision making will send an unmistakable message to agencies that Congress considers agency performance a priority.

Over the years, the Committee on Homeland Security and Governmental Affairs and its predecessors have done commendable work focusing attention on improving government management and performance—by reporting out legislation, such as the original GPRA and GPRAMA, and through hearings, such as this one. Moving forward, congressional oversight and sustained attention by top administration officials will be essential to ensure further improvement in the performance of federal programs and operations. In fact, as we noted in our recent high-risk issues report, these two factors were absolutely critical to making the progress necessary for the DOD Personnel Security Clearance Program and the 2010 Census to be removed from our high-risk list.[19]

GAO's Role in Evaluating GPRAMA, High Risks, and Other Major Government Challenges

Realizing the promise of GPRAMA for improving government performance and accountability and reducing waste will require sustained oversight of implementation. GAO played a major role in evaluating the implementation of the original GPRA's strategic and annual performance planning requirements including various pilot provisions. For example, by evaluating agency plans during a pilot phase, we were able to offer numerous recommendations for improvement that led to more effective final plans.[20] We further supported implementation by reporting on leading management practices that agencies should employ as they implemented GPRA.[21] It is worth noting that much of our work on government performance has been conducted at the request of the Committee on Homeland Security and Governmental Affairs and your two subcommittees, showing a sustained commitment to ensure GPRA was effectively implemented.

Similarly, GPRAMA includes provisions requiring GAO to review implementation of the act at several critical junctures, and provide recommendations for improvements to implementation of the act. First, following a period of initial implementation, by June 2013, GAO is to report on implementation of the act's planning and reporting requirements—at both the governmentwide and agency levels. Subsequently, following full implementation, by September 2015 and 2017, GAO is to evaluate whether performance management is being used by federal agencies to improve the efficiency and effectiveness of agency programs. Also in September 2015 and 2017—and every 4 years thereafter—GAO is to evaluate the implementation of the federal government priority goals and performance plans, and related reporting required by the act.

Looking ahead, a number of other required recurrent reports will help to inform Congress about government management and performance. For example, GAO has an ongoing statutory requirement to report each year on federal programs, agencies, offices, and initiatives, either within departments or governmentwide, which have duplicative goals or activities.[22] In addition, each year GAO reports on its audit of the consolidated financial statements of the U.S. government[23] and the condition of federal financial management systems.[24] GAO continues to report periodically to Congress on the adequacy and effectiveness of agencies' information security policies and practices and other requirements of the Federal Information Security Management Act of 2002.[25]

Additionally, the Presidential Transition Act of 2000[26] identifies GAO as a source of briefings and other materials to help inform presidential appointees of the major management issues, risks, and challenges they will face. During the last presidential transition, we identified for Congress and the new administration urgent issues and key program and management challenges in the major departments and across government. Finally, GAO reports to each new Congress on government operations that it identifies as high risk due to their greater vulnerabilities to fraud, waste, abuse, and mismanagement or the need for broad-based transformation to address economy, efficiency, or effectiveness challenges.

In conclusion, everything must be on the table as we address the federal long-term fiscal challenge. While the long-term outlook is driven on the spending side of the budget by rising health care costs and demographics, other areas of the budget should not be exempt from scrutiny. All areas should be reexamined in light of the contributions they make to achieving outcomes for the American public. If programs are overlapping, fragmented, or duplicative, they must be streamlined. Programs and management functions at significant risk of waste, fraud, and abuse must be corrected. GPRAMA provides the administration and Congress with new tools to identify strategies that are achieving results as well as those that are ineffective, duplicative, or wasteful that could be eliminated. GAO stands ready to help Congress ensure that the act's promises are met.

Thank you, Chairmen Akaka and Carper, Ranking Members Johnson and Brown, and Members of the Subcommittees. This concludes my prepared statement. I would be pleased to answer any questions you may have.

APPENDIX I: GPRA MODERNIZATION ACT OF 2010 IMPLEMENTATION

Implementation of Selected Requirements Provided in the GPRA Modernization Act of 2010

Key Date	Implementation Requirement
June 30, 2011	Agency quarterly priority progress reviews, consistent with the requirements of the act, begin for the goals contained in the Fiscal Year 2011 Budget of the United States Government.
Key Date	Implementation Requirement
February 6, 2012	OMB publishes interim federal government priority goals and prepares and submits a federal government performance plan consistent with the requirements of the act. Agencies adjust their current strategic plans, prepare and submit performance plans, and identify new or update existing agency priority goals to make them consistent with the requirements of the act.
No later than February 27, 2012	Agencies make performance reporting updates on their fiscal year 2011 performance consistent with the requirements of the act.

Key Date	Implementation Requirement
June 30, 2012	OMB begins federal government quarterly priority progress reviews.
No later than October 1, 2012	OMB launches a single governmentwide performance website.
February 3, 2014	Full implementation of the act with a new strategic planning cycle.

End Notes

[1] Pub. L. No. 111-352, 124 Stat. 3866 (2011). GPRAMA amends the Government Performance and Results Act of 1993, Pub. L. No. 103-62, 107 Stat. 285 (1993).

[2] GAO, *Government Performance: GPRA Modernization Act Provides Opportunities to Help Address Fiscal, Performance, and Management Challenges*, GAO-11-466T (Washington, D.C.: Mar. 16, 2011).

[3] GAO, *The Federal Government's Long-Term Fiscal Outlook: January 2011 Update*, GAO-11-451SP (Washington, D.C.: Mar. 17, 2010). GAO updates these simulations twice each year. Updates and additional information on the federal fiscal outlook, federal debt, and the outlook for state and local government sector is available at: www.gao.gov/special.pubs/longterm/.

[4] GAO, *Opportunities to Reduce Potential Duplication in Government Programs, Save Tax Dollars, and Enhance Revenue*, GAO-11-318SP (Washington, D.C.: Mar. 1, 2011). An interactive, Web-based version of the report is available at: http://www.gao.gov/ereport/gao-11-318SP.

[5] GAO, *High-Risk Series: An Update*, GAO-11-278 (Washington, D.C.: February 2011). Additional information available on GAO's High-Risk and Other Major Government Challenges Web site, http://www.gao.gov/highrisk.

[6] The Patient Protection and Affordable Care Act established a Commission on Key NationalIndicators that will enter into an arrangement with the National Academy of Sciences to establish a U.S. key national indicator system. Pub. L. No. 111-148, § 5605, 124 Stat. 119, 680–684 (2010).

[7] GAO, *Key Indicator Systems: Experiences of Other National and Subnational Systems Offer Insights for the United States*, GAO-11-396 (Washington, D.C.: Mar. 31, 2011).

[8] GAO, *Opportunities to Reduce Potential Duplication in Federal Teacher Quality Programs*, GAO-11-510T (Washington, D.C.: Apr. 13, 2011).

[9] GAO, *Employment and Training Programs: Opportunities Exist for Improving Efficiency*, GAO-11-506T (Washington: D.C.: Apr. 7, 2011).

[10] 31 U.S.C. § 1120(a)(1)(B).

[11] More information on our work related to challenges in these five management functions isavailable at http://www.gao.gov/highrisk/challenges/.

[12] GAO-11-318SP.

[13] GAO, *Results-Oriented Government: GPRA Has Established a Solid Foundation for Achieving Greater Results*, GAO-04-38 (Washington, D.C.: Mar. 10, 2004).

[14] GAO, *Government Performance: Lessons Learned for the Next Administration on Using Performance Information to Improve Results*, GAO-08-1026T (Washington, D.C.: July 24, 2008).

[15] GAO-04-38.

[16] OMB, *Analytical Perspectives, Budget of the United States Government, Fiscal Year 2012*, p. 79.

[17] OMB described PART, which was created in 2002, as a diagnostic tool meant to provide a consistent approach to evaluating federal programs as part of the executive budget formulation process.

[18] GAO, *Performance Budgeting: PART Focuses Attention on Program Performance, but More Can Be Done to Engage Congress*, GAO-06-28 (Washington, D.C.: Oct. 28, 2005).

[19] GAO-11-278.

[20] See for example, GAO, *Managing for Results: Critical Issues for Improving Federal Agencies' Strategic Plans*, GAO/GGD-97-180 (Washington, D.C.: Sept.16, 1997) and *Managing for Results: An Agenda to Improve the Usefulness of Agencies' Annual Performance Plans*, GAO/GGD/AIMD-98-228 (Washington, D.C.: Sept. 8, 1998).

[21] See for example, GAO, *Executive Guide: Effectively Implementing the Government Performance and Results Act*, GAO/GGD-96-118 (Washington, D.C.: June 1996).

[22] Pub. L. No. 111-139, § 21, 124 Stat. 8, 29 (2010), 31 U.S.C. § 712 note.

[23] 31 U.S.C. § 331(e)(2).

[24] 31 U.S.C. § 3512 note.

[25] E-Government Act of 2002, Pub. L. No. 107-347, Title III, 116 Stat. 2899, 2946 (2002).

[26] Pub. L. No. 106-293, §2(3), 114 Stat. 1035 (2000).

In: Modernization of the Government … ISBN: 978-1-62257-383-7
Editors: R. Hawkins and T. P. Duncan

Chapter 3

GPRA MODERNIZATION ACT OF 2010*

Senate Committee on Homeland Security and Governmental Affairs

The Committee on Homeland Security and Governmental Affairs, to which was referred the bill (H.R. 2142) to require quarterly performance assessments of Government programs for purposes of assessing agency performance and improvement, and to establish agency performance improvement officers and the Performance Im provement Council, having considered the same, reports favorably thereon with an amendment in the nature of a substitute, and recommends that the bill, as amended, do pass.

I. PURPOSE AND SUMMARY

The Government Performance and Results Act of 1993[1] (GPRA) created a thorough and comprehensive framework for federal government strategic planning and performance reporting. Since its enactment, GPRA has helped improve the efficiency and effectiveness of federal programs by requiring that agencies establish a system to set goals for program performance and measure results.

However GPRA needs to be improved and updated to take advantage of the latest technologies and to apply lessons learned from nearly two decades of

---

* This is an edited, reformatted and augmented version of Senate Committee on Homeland Security and Governmental Affairs, Publication No. 111–372, dated December 16, 2010.

implementation. H.R. 2142 will modernize and refine the requirements established by GPRA in order to produce more frequent, relevant data which can then inform deci sion makers and agency operations.

II. BACKGROUND AND NEED FOR THE LEGISLATION

During the 103rd Congress, this Committee acted on concerns— among its members as well as the public—that the federal government was not working as well as it should.[2] Sharing the public's frustration and following its previous legislative and oversight work to address waste, inefficiency, and ineffectiveness in federal programs, the Committee considered S. 20, the Government Per formance and Results Act (GPRA). At the time, the Committee be lieved that the regular and systemic measurement and reporting of program performance, compared to preestablished goals, would be valuable to the federal government (including Congress) and pro vide a beneficial supplement to the Committee's previous work in the area of management improvement.[3]

GPRA sought to promote greater efficiency, effectiveness, and ac countability in federal spending by establishing a new framework for performance management and budgeting in federal agencies. Additionally, GPRA was intended to improve congressional decision making by providing objective information on the relative efficiency and effectiveness of federal programs and spending.[4] The law re quires three types of ongoing planning, evaluation, and reporting requirements for executive branch agencies: strategic plans, annual performance plans, and annual reports on program performance. It also requires that agencies consult with Congress when developing a strategic plan, and consider views of other interested stake holders. GPRA implementation, combined with other statutory ef forts in the 1990s addressing longstanding management prob lems,[5] has provided a powerful framework for developing and inte grating information about agencies' strategic priorities, the results oriented performance goals that flow from those priorities, perform ance data to show the level of achievement of those goals, and the relationship of reliable and audited financial information and infor mation technology investments to the achievement of those goals.[6]

In 2004, after a decade of implementation, Congress asked the Government Accountability Office (GAO) to assess GPRA. The re sulting report concluded that the statutory requirements under GPRA "have established a solid foundation of resultsoriented per formance planning, measurement, and reporting in federal government."[7] However, GAO also found serious weaknesses in the im plementation of GPRA, such as the lack of detail in required plans on how performance goals relate to strategic goals. Additionally, GAO found that agencies were not coordinating their efforts in order to address common challenges and achieve common objec tives.[8] GAO noted that such mission fragmentation and overlap among agencies makes it particularly difficult to address cross cutting national issues, such as homeland security, drug control, and the environment.[9] Finally, GAO also found that timing issues may hinder the development of useful agency strategic plans. Spe cifically, agencies are often required to update strategic plans just before a presidential election and without input from a new Con gress. If a new president is elected, the updated plan is essentially moot and does not have the commitment and sustained attention of top leadership within the agency.[10]

H.R. 2142 addresses these weaknesses by amending GPRA to: re quire the Office of Management and Budget to provide government wide priority goals; increase the frequency and enhance quality of agency reporting; and improve the transparency of performance re porting. The bill also improves federal performance management by establishing a Chief Operating Officer (COO) within each agency tasked with improving the performance of his or her agency. It also codifies and strengthens the existing resources for performance management, including the Performance Improvement Officers (PIOs) within the federal agencies and the interagency Perform ance Improvement Council (PIC).[11]

Agency Strategic Plans

Strategic plans are the starting point and basic underpinning for a system of program goalsetting and performance measurement that will be established throughout the federal government. A multi-year strategic plan articulates the fundamental mission (or missions) of an organization, and lays out its long-term general goals for implementing that mission, including the resources need ed to reach these goals.[12] GPRA requires agencies to develop stra tegic plans with long-term outcomeoriented goals and objectives, annual goals linked to achieving the long-term goals, and annual reports on the goals achieved. Under GPRA, an agency is currently required to develop a strategic plan at least every three years to cover the following five year period. This reporting timeframe for updating strategic plans does not correspond to presidential terms. It makes little sense to require an update of a strategic plan short ly before a new administration is scheduled to take office, as changes in political leadership often result in new objectives and can render preexisting plans unuseful.

H.R. 2142 addresses this issue by modifying the schedule for re vising agency strategic plans to align with presidential terms. The bill requires strategic plans cover a period of no less than four years and allows the agency to make adjustments to the plan to re flect significant changes in its operating environment, with appropriate notification to Congress. This is not to mean that an agency should frequently modify its existing strategic plans; rather the in tent of this change is to provide agencies the flexibility to respond to an event that significantly changes the operating environment.

This legislation also amends existing GPRA requirements for the contents of an agency strategic plan. As specified in the law and subsequent guidance from the Office of Management and Budget (OMB) and GAO, an agency's strategic plan must contain six key components:

- a comprehensive agency mission statement;
- agencywide long-term goals and objectives for all major functions and operations;
- approaches or strategies to achieve the goals and objec tives and the various resources needed;
- a description of the relationship between the long-term goals and objectives and the annual performance goals;
- an identification of key factors, external to the agency and beyond its control, that could significantly affect the achieve ment of the strategic goals; and
- a description of how program evaluations were used to es tablish or revise strategic goals, and a schedule for future pro gram evaluations.[13]

H.R. 2142 requires agencies to describe how any goals and objec tives in its strategic plan contribute to the cross-cutting federal gov ernment priority goals required by this legislation. This mandate seeks to ensure that agency goals align with broader federal efforts on that mission, and to provide greater clarity regarding the im pact of employee efforts on overarching goals.

Across the federal government, various agencies operate similar or related programs. GAO has found that mission fragmentation and program overlap are widespread across the government and that addressing this challenge is essential to the success of national strategies in areas such as homeland security, drug control, and the environment.[14] Without appropriate coordination, such pro grams may be implemented in a fragmented manner which wastes scarce resources, confuses citizens, and limits the overall effective ness of the federal effort. H.R. 2142 requires an agency to describe how it is working with other agencies to achieve its own goals and objectives, as well as the cross-cutting priority goals of the federal government.

One of the original goals of GPRA was to strengthen the collabo ration between Congress and the federal agencies to improve gov ernment performance. For its part, Congress needs more objective information on the relative effectiveness and efficiency of federal programs and spending. The Committee expressed the importance of Congressional consultation in its report on GPRA in 1993: "par ticularly during this time of very tight budget constraints, it is im portant that Congress develop a clear understanding of what it is getting in the way of results from each dollar spent, and how those results would change with an increase or decrease in funding. In all likelihood, Congress will face difficult, wrenching budget deci sions for years to come. But even if the budget were balanced, and revenues strong, this information would be important in the mak ing of wise spending decisions."[15]

GPRA also established a consultation process so that agencies could take Congressional views into account as appropriate. How ever, little evidence exists that agencies have formally or significantly considered the input of key stakeholders when developing goals and objectives. In waiting to consult with relevant congres sional stakeholders until a strategic plan has been substantially drafted and vetted within the executive branch, agencies forego im portant opportunities to learn early on about specific concerns that will be critical to successful implementation. Therefore, this Com mittee again strongly emphasizes that Congressional consultations are to take place during the development of the plan—not after.

H.R. 2142 strengthens the Congressional consultation process by encouraging agencies to describe how agency goals and objectives incorporate the views and suggestions obtained through consulta tions with Congress. This legislation clarifies that the agency shall periodically consult with and obtain majority and minority views from its authorizing, appropriations, and oversight committees when developing or making adjustments to its strategic plan. It also requires Congressional consultations occur at least once every two years; this is to ensure that each Congress has input on the goals, objectives, strategies, and performance measures of the agen cy. Moreover, it allows the agency to have an opportunity to pro vide a progress report on its performance and ensures that various committees are getting the types of performance information they need.

Agency Performance Plans

Building on the decisions made as part of the strategic planning process, GPRA requires executive agencies to develop annual per formance plans covering each program activity in the agencies' budgets. Each plan should contain an agency's annual performance goals and associated measures to gauge its progress toward its strategic goals. OMB should then incorporate these performance plans to develop an overall federal government performance plan that will be submitted with the President's budget. The overall plan is intended to present Congress with a single cohesive picture of the federal government's annual performance goals for a given fiscal year.[16]

GAO has stated that a clear relationship should exist between an agency's long-term strategic goals and mission and the performance goals in the annual performance plan.[17] H.R. 2142 requires an agency to describe how the performance goals contained in its per formance plan contribute to the goals and objectives established in the agency's strategic plan, as well as any overall federal government performance goals. Additionally, this legislation requires that an agency's performance plan cover a twoyear period, including both the current fiscal year and the next one. Under existing law, an agency's performance plan is only required to cover the next fis cal year. Adding the current year requirement will enable an agen cy to update its current year goals, milestones, and strategies to re flect actual resources and any changes in the operating environ ment that differ from what was expected when the original plan was submitted the previous year. This, in turn, will provide a more uptodate context for evaluating the goals for the upcoming fiscal year.

The key to improving performance accountability is to document the results agencies have achieved compared to the goals they have established. Therefore, H.R. 2142 requires an agency to provide ad ditional information about how the agency plans to achieve its per formance goals by identifying clearly defined milestones, the agen cy officials responsible for ensuring each goal is achieved, and the program activities, regulations, policies and other activities that support each goal. Without a clear description of the strategies and resources an agency plans to use, it will be difficult for Congress to assess the likelihood of the agency's success in achieving its in tended results.[18] By describing the strategies to be used to achieve results and the resources to be applied to those strategies, the per formance plan can help Congress understand and assess the rela tionship between the agency's resources and results. Credible performance information is essential for accurately as sessing an agency's progress towards its goals and, in cases where goals are not met, identifying opportunities for improvement or whether goals need to be adjusted. In order to improve the credi bility of performance data, H.R. 2142 requires an agency to provide additional information about how it will ensure the validity and re liability of such data. Performance plans must also analyze how program activities con tribute to the agency's mission and goals. Inevitably, some program activities may not contribute or have limited contributions to an agency's annual performance goals and will be designated as low priority program activities. The Committee expects that agencies will take actions to address these lowpriority program activities, which could include retooling the program activities where author ized, requesting legislative changes to improve the program activi ties, or proposing their termination or consolidation with any simi lar program activities.

H.R. 2142 requires agencies to provide a performance update at least annually, occurring no later than 150 days after the end of the fiscal year. However, agencies are encouraged to provide more frequent updates that would provide significant value to the federal government, Congress, or other key stakeholders. This legislation also requires the agency to post its performance plan on the agency website concurrent with the submission of the budget for the United States Government. This is a change from the existing GPRA requirement that the plans simply be submitted to the President and Congress.

H.R. 2142 addresses an omission from the original GPRA law, which did not specify how or where agencies should report on the performance of any classified activities, even though it did allow for a classified annex. To this end, the bill clearly requires that agen cies provide performance updates for classified program activities in the classified appendix of the agency performance plan.

Federal Government Performance Plan and Priority Goals

In its ten year review of GPRA, GAO recommended that Con gress require the development of a government-wide strategic plan in order to provide a framework for identifying long-term goals and strategies to address issues that cut across federal agencies.[19] Such a plan would provide a cohesive perspective on the long-term goals of the federal government and provide a much needed basis for fully integrating, rather than merely coordinating, a wide array of federal activities. In the past, OMB has noted that the budget serves as a government strategic plan. However, this Committee agrees with GAO's assessment that the President's Budget focuses on establishing agency budgets for the upcoming fiscal year and provides neither a long-term nor an integrated perspective on fed eral government activities.[20] Rather than explicitly requiring such a strategic plan, H.R. 2142 enhances the existing requirements for a federal government performance plan, establishes the develop ment of federal government priority goals, and requires agencies to have their own priority goals in order to achieve those federal gov ernment priority goals. These three important measures, alongside requirements for quarterly progress reviews and webbased report ing, set up a government-wide strategic and planning process.

Federal Government Performance Plan: GPRA currently requires that beginning with the fiscal year 1999 budget submission, the an nual budget of the U.S. Government include a federal government performance plan. The plan was intended to present a single cohe sive picture of the federal government's annual performance goal for the fiscal year. GPRA allows the plan to be integrated with the detailed budget estimates, appear as an individual part of the main budget document, or be submitted separately. Additionally, this Committee intended that the performance plan be submitted coin cident with the principal budget documents so that Congress would have this plan available when reviewing the agency budget esti mates.[21] Under the law, the Director of OMB (the Director) has discretion in determining the best manner and most useful format for submitting the performance plan. However, OMB has not opted to issue a distinct federal government performance plan since fiscal year 1999. In that year, GAO found that the federal government performance plan was a derivative document that compiled agency level plans and reflected budget and management decisions made throughout the process of formulating the President's budget sub mission.[22]

H.R. 2142 stresses the importance of a federal government per formance plan and enhances requirements for the plan to address cross-cutting program efforts. Focusing broadly on government-wide outcomes should be a central and distinguishing feature of the fed eral government performance plan.[23] The bill requires that:

- the plan establish performance goals for each cross-cutting federal government priority goal;

- OMB identify the various agencies, organizations, program activities, regulations, tax expenditures, policies and other ac tivities that contribute to each federal government performance goal;
- a lead government official be assigned for each federal gov ernment performance goal;
- OMB establish common federal government performance indicators to measure and assess progress across agencies to ward shared goals; and
- OMB identify government and crossagency management challenges and plans to address such challenges.

Federal Priority Goals: H.R. 2142 also establishes requirements for federal government priority goals. Unfortunately, GPRA compli ance currently is largely an independent exercise among agencies, with agency performance plans largely focused on goals directly re lated to agency statutory missions. H.R. 2142 requires the Director of OMB to work with agencies to develop federal government pri ority goals that aim to improve performance and management across the federal government. The cross-cutting policy goals are re quired to be outcomeoriented and limited in number to ensure that there is ample focus on achieving these goals over time. The man agementrelated goals should cover management functions where significant improvements are needed across the federal government, such as information technology, human capital, and financial management. Recognizing that achieving the federal government priority goals will require sustained focus over a period of time, the goals are required to be long-term in nature and updated or revised at least every four years. Under H.R. 2142 the Director is able to make adjustments to the goals should there be significant changes in the federal government's operating environment. However, the Committee expects that many of these goals will stay constant over time, including across Administrations, since these challenges are not likely to be overcome during a four year period.

Successful strategic planning requires the involvement of key stakeholders. This collaboration can serve as a mechanism for building consensus and provides a vehicle for the President to ar ticulate long-term goals and a road map for achieving them.[24]

Therefore, when developing or adjusting the goals, and at least once each Congress, the Director is required to consult with key congressional committees and obtain both majority and minority views on the draft goals.

The federal government priority goals should complement the federal government performance plan, effectively functioning as a government-wide strategic plan. This legislation also addresses the need to increase transparency by providing a process for developing the federal government priority goals and making them available to the public. H.R. 2142 requires that the goals be developed or re vised at least once every four years and be made publicly available concurrently with the submission of the budget of the United States Government in the second year of a President's term. At a minimum, the Committee expects the goals will be posted on the government-wide performance website provided for in this legisla tion.

Agency Priority Goals: In order for the federal government to make progress towards and eventually achieve its priority goals, agencies must align their goals with those of the federal government. H.R. 2142 requires the head of each agency[25] to identify agency priority goals from among the agency's performance goals. The Director of OMB would have authority to determine the total number of agency priority goals across the federal government, as well as the number of priority goals to be developed by each agency. The Committee expects the total number of federal goals will not exceed 100 and agency goals will not exceed five per agency, while acknowledging variation may exist depending on the size and mission of a given agency.

As the name implies, agency priority goals should reflect the agency's highest priorities, as determined by the head of the agen cy. Such goals should be informed by any federal government pri ority goals to which the agency contributes.

The priority goals have a two year timeframe, with ambitious but achievable performance targets and milestones. These should be "stretch" goals—the agency should set the goal to exceed its normal level of performance, but within reasonable reach. Although the language of the bill states that the goals are to be achievable, the Committee under stands that external factors may cause agencies to fall short at times and a certain percentage of missed goals is acceptable. Since agency will likely select some complex and long-term challenges as target for improvement, the Committee expects that many priority goals will continue from a given two year cycle to the next, with updated performance targets and milestones all leading to a clearly defined end state.

As with each of the agency's other performance goals, each priority goal should have a clearly identified leader who is responsible for reaching the given goal.

Establishing AgencyLevel Chief Operation Officer

In 2002, GAO convened a roundtable to discuss the Chief Oper ation Officer (COO) concept and how it might apply within federal agencies as one strategy to address certain systemic federal govern ance and management challenges.

Participants generally agreed that agency COOs could help increase attention to management issues and transformational change, integrate various key manage ment and transformation efforts, and institutionalize accountability for addressing management issues and leading transformational change.[26]

Two Presidential memoranda—one on October 1, 1993 and an update on July 11, 2001—outlined a COO position within the federal government.[27] Both memoranda provided the COO with re sponsibilities to improve the management and performance of the agency, and implement the agency mission and goals.

H.R. 2142 keeps those responsibilities and adds others to bring them in line with the planning and reporting requirements provided in this leg islation. H.R. 2142 would codify that the deputy head of an agency, or equivalent, shall be an agency's COO and given overall responsi bility for improving the management and performance of the agency.

The COO would also assist the head of the agency in carrying out the planning and reporting requirements of this bill, oversee agencyspecific efforts to improve management within the agency and across the federal government, and coordinate with relevant personnel within and external to the agency who have a significant role in contributing to the mission and goals of the agency.[28]

Both Presidential Memoranda mentioned above also established the President's Management Council (PMC), led by the Deputy Di rector for Management of OMB and composed of various agency COOs. The PMC has general responsibilities aimed at improving federal government management. Although H.R. 2142 does not cod ify the PMC, the Committee expects that the management council will continue to exist and continue to be responsible for improving management across the federal government.

The PMC could also play an important role in ensuring that relevant agencies and other interagency councils effectively coordinate efforts to achieve the federal government priority goals.

Establishing AgencyLevel Performance Improvement Officer and the Performance Improvement Council

H.R. 2142 also establishes in statute the position of a Perform ance Improvement Officer (PIO) at each agency. The PIO position currently exists in the federal government, having been established by *Executive Order (E.O.) 13450, Improving Government Program Performance,* on November 13, 2007.[29] Although the bill codifies parts of the Executive Order into statute, it also makes changes to the responsibilities of a PIO in order to align the position with planning and reporting requirements provided in this legislation.

H.R. 2142 directs the head of each agency to designate a senior executive of the agency as the agency PIO. In requiring that the PIO be selected from among the agency's senior executives, the bill attempts to ensure continuity for this position over time in order to help the agency focus on achieving its long-term goals. This long term focus is especially important because the tenure of political appointees in top leadership positions within an agency usually lasts only a few years.

The bill also establishes in statute a government-wide Perform ance Improvement Council (PIC), comprising the Deputy Director for Management of OMB, who serves as the chairperson, the PIOs from each of the 24 CFO Act agencies, other agency PIOs and other individuals as determined appropriate by the chairperson. The PIC was originally established under E.O. 13450. H.R. 2142 enhances the responsibilities of the PIC, directing it to coordinate perform ance and management activities with other interagency manage ment councils.[30] The Committee expects that other interagency management councils will take lead responsibility for implementing the management improvementrelated federal government priority goals (i.e., the Chief Financial Officers Council will be responsible for the financial managementrelated goal), with the PIC assisting the other councils and monitoring progress toward the goals.

Reviewing Federal Government and Agency Priority Goals

H.R. 2142 attempts to lay out a process for reviewing progress towards the federal government priority goals on, at minimum, a quarterly basis. For each federal government priority goal, the Di rector of OMB should review the progress achieved during the most recent quarter and the likelihood of meeting the performance tar get. As a part of these reviews, the Director of OMB and the PIC must categorize the federal government priority goals according to the risk of not meeting performance targets, and for those at great est risk, identify strategies to improve performance.

The Director of OMB and the PIC are also required to assess whether the agencies, organizations, program activities, regula tions, tax expenditures, policies and other activities are contrib uting as planned to each federal government priority. By looking at the contribution of each underlying federal entity and type of federal intervention, the Director of OMB and the PIC may be able to identify successful practices that could be replicated by other agencies to improve their results and contributions to the overall federal government priority goal. This assessment process may also reveal federal activities that are duplicative or even working at crosspurposes.

H.R. 2142 provides an analogous review process at each agency required to develop priority goals. For each agency priority goal, the head of the agency and the COO, with the support of the agency PIO, reviews the progress achieved during the most recent quar ter and the likelihood of meeting the performance target. The re views should include the designated leader for each agency priority goal, and relevant personnel within and external to the agency. The reviews should also highlight and strategize regarding high risk areas—in other word, where there is the greatest risk of not meeting a priority goal. Further, the head of the agency, COO, and PIO must assess whether the relevant organizations, program ac tivities, regulations, policies and other activities are contributing as planned to each agency priority.

This approach is aimed at increasing the use of performance in formation to improve performance and results. Through government-wide surveys of federal managers between 1997 and 2007, GAO found that although federal managers reported they had more performance measures in 2007 than in 1997, their reported use of the performance information collected by those measures had not changed significantly during that ten year period.[31] Agencies are collecting a significant amount of information, but are not consist ently using that information to improve their management and results.

Webbased Reporting

This legislation requires OMB to develop a single government wide performance website by 2012 that will feature performance in formation outlined in the bill and provided by the agency. The bill further requires that OMB issue guidance to agencies on providing performance information for publication on this website. In addi tion, agencies are required to produce all strategic plans, perform ance plans, and performance reports in searchable, machineread able formats beginning in fiscal year 2012.

H.R. 2142 also attempts to reduce unnecessary and duplicative printed reports by prohibiting the printing of strategic plans, per formance plans, and performance reports for external release, ex cept when being provided to Congress. The public will be able to access these plans and reports on the government-wide perform ance website established in this bill.

H.R. 2142 additionally requires each agency's COO to compile a list of all plans and reports the agency produces for Congress, ei ther by law or as directed in congressional reports, and identify outdated or duplicative requirements. The bill then provides that the President submit to Congress, concurrent with the submission of the budget of the United States government, a list of the plans and reports that the agencies identified as outdated or duplicative and authorizes the Director of OMB to concurrently submit a legis lative proposal to eliminate or consolidate these outdated and du plicative plans.

Office of Personnel Management

GPRA previously required the Office of Personnel Management (OPM) to develop a strategic planning and performance measure ment training component for its management training program. In a 2007 survey of federal managers, GAO found that since 1997, while there has been a significant increase in training, only about half of GAO's survey respondents in 2007 reported receiving any training that would assist in strategic planning and performance assessment.[32]

H.R. 2142 calls for the Director of OPM, in consultation with the PIC, to identify key skills and competencies related to performance management in the federal government. This is an important step to ensure that agencies are able to train their personnel to effec tively use performance measurement building capabilities for con tinued performance planning. It is essential to build analytical ca pacity to use performance information and to ensure its quality in order to use that performance information in a meaningful fashion to improve government. GAO has previously noted the value of providing training on setting program performance goals and the use of performance information, and recommended that OMB ensure that agencies are making adequate investments in such training.[33]

This requirement will help ensure that relevant agency personnel have access to such training.

Implementation

One reason GPRA differed from prior performance initiatives is that it was phased in over time. The federal government perform ance initiatives that preceded GPRA were typically implemented government-wide within a single year. GPRA, in contrast, provided a multi-year and iterative government-wide implementation process that incorporated pilot tests and formal evaluations of key con cepts. In this manner, GPRA increased the potential for integration of planning, budgeting, and performance measurement while guarding against the unreasonably high expectations that plagued earlier initiatives.[34] H.R. 2142 continues this successful aspect of GPRA by providing timeframes for implementing this Act, includ ing interim planning and reporting activities. In addition, the bill requires GAO to evaluate interim activities and recommend im provements for full implementation.

Congressional Oversight and Legislation

H.R. 2142 reiterates a clause from GPRA that nothing in this Act shall be construed as limiting Congress' ability to establish, amend, suspend, or annul, any federal government or agency goals. In ad dition, the bill provides for several GAO reviews of this Act's imple mentation over time. The Committee expects that in addition to identifying needed improvements and making recommendations to enhance implementation, GAO will identify in these reports prom ising practices found at certain agencies that could be replicated at other agencies to improve their results and performance manage ment.

Inherently Governmental Functions

This Committee notes that while H.R. 2142 seeks to modernize and refine key aspects of GPRA, the statutory foundation estab lished by GPRA remains intact. The enactment of GPRA marked a key moment in federal government performance management ini tiatives by elevating management to a priority for both the Execu tive Branch and Congress. This Committee was the prime mover behind the development and passage of GPRA in 1993, and the Committee has taken great care to protect GPRA provisions proven to be beneficial and effective over the years. This bill makes tar geted amendments to specific parts of GPRA, while leaving many GPRA provisions, and the accompanying Congressional intent, in tact and unchanged. The Committee recognizes that the Congres sional intent behind GPRA provisions left unchanged or modified for technical and conforming reasons (including where the Com mittee extended existing GPRA standards to apply to new components established by H.R. 2142 that did not exist in 1993) will con tinue to apply as it has since the enactment of GPRA in 1993.

For example, the Committee chose not to change the language and accompanying Congressional intent of the GPRA provisions that declare the preparation of an agency strategic plan, annual performance plan, or annual program performance report, to be an inherently governmental function. The GPRA Committee Report defines this as a "function that is so intimately related to the pub lic interest as to mandate performance by Government employees," while clearly stating that although GPRA specifies government em ployees are solely to be responsible for the final plan or report, this does not limit agencies from being assisted by nonfederal parties, such as contractors or grantees, in the preparation of these plans and reports.[35] Thus, the 1993 GPRA standards addressing the issue of inherently governmental functions have simply been ex tended to apply to the inherently governmental provisions in H.R. 2142, located in section 306(e) of title 5, United States Code, as well as sections 1115(f), 1116(e), and 1120(c) of title 31, United States Code."[36]

III. Legislative History

Representative Henry Cuellar introduced H.R. 2142 in the House of Representatives on April 28, 2009. The House passed H.R. 2142 on June 16, 2010 by voice vote.

On June 17, 2010, H.R. 2142 was received in the Senate, read twice, and referred to the Committee on Homeland Security and Governmental Affairs. On September 29, 2010 the Committee con sidered the measure, and Senator Carper offered an amendment in the nature of a substitute, which was adopted by voice vote. The Committee then adopted the bill as amended by voice vote and or dered it favorably reported to the Senate. Members present for the vote on the substitute amendment, and the vote on the bill as amended, were

Senators Lieberman, Collins, Akaka, Carper, Pryor, Tester, Burris, Kaufman, and Brown.

IV. Section by Section Analysis

Section 1. Short title

This section provides the short title of the bill, the GPRA Mod ernization Act of 2010.

Section 2. Strategic planning amendments

This section requires federal agencies to post their strategic plan on the agency's website no later than the first Monday in February in the second year of a Presidential term.

This section also revises the schedule for agency strategic plans to align with presidential terms.

In addition, this section sets out requirements for the contents of an agency's strategic plan, including a comprehensive mission statement and general goals and objectives.

The agency is also re quired to describe in its strategic plan how any goals and objectives in its plan contribute to the cross-cutting federal government pri ority goals added by section 5 of the bill and to describe how the goals and objectives incorporate the views and suggestions obtained through Congressional consultations.

Strategic plans are required to cover a period of no less than four years and this section allows the agency to make adjustments to the plan to reflect significant changes in its operating environment, with appropriate notification of Congress.

In addition, this section requires the agency to consult with and obtain majority and minor ity views from the relevant authorizing, appropriations, and over sight committees when developing or making adjustments to its strategic plan; these congressional consultations are required to occur at least once every two years.

The agency must also consider the views of other key stakeholders.

Section 3. Performance Planning Amendments

This section amends section 1115 of title 31, U.S. Code, which is retitled "Federal Government and Agency Performance Plans."

This section expands on the existing GPRA requirement for a federal government performance plan. It requires the Director of OMB to coordinate with agencies to develop the plan, which (1) es tablishes performance goals for each federal government priority goal; (2) identifies the various agencies, organizations, program ac tivities, regulations, tax expenditures, policies, and other activities that contribute to each federal government performance goal; (3) identifies a lead government official for each federal government performance goal; (4) establishes common federal government per formance indicators to measure and assess progress; and (5) identi fies government-wide and crossagency major management chal lenges and plans to address such challenges.

This section also requires the agency to post its performance plan on the agency website concurrent with the submission of the budg et for the United States Government. The agency performance plan is to include performance goals for both the fiscal year in which the plan is submitted as well as the next fiscal year.

In addition, this section requires the agency to describe how the performance goals contained in the plan contribute to the goals and objectives established in the agency's strategic plan, as well as any federal government performance goals contained in the federal gov ernment performance plan. The agency is required to identify which, if any, performance goals are designated as agency priority goals. It must also explain how the agency plans to achieve its per formance goals, including by identifying clearly defined milestones; agency officials—referred to as goal leaders—responsible for ensur ing each goal is achieved; the human, capital and information re sources required to meet the performance goals; and the organiza tions program activities, regulations, policies and other activities that support each goal. The agency must also describe how it is col laborating and coordinating with other agencies to achieve its per formance goal as well as relevant federal government performance goals.

This section amends an existing requirement and directs agen cies to develop a balanced set of performance indicators to measure or assess progress toward each performance goal, including cus tomer service, efficiency, output, and outcome indicators. It also re quires agencies to provide additional information about how it will ensure the validity and reliability of its performance data. Further, it requires the agency to identify its major management challenges and identify how it plans to address those challenges.

This section also requires the agency to identify lowpriority pro gram activities based on an analysis of the program activities' con tribution to the agency's mission and goals.

If an agency, in consultation with the Director of OMB, deter mines that it is not feasible to express the performance goals for a particular program activity in an objective, quantifiable, and measurable form, this section allows the Director of OMB to au thorize an alternative form. Such an alternative program must in clude detailed information that would allow for an accurate, inde pendent determination of whether the program activity's perform ance is a minimally effective program or a successful program.

This section also provides new definitions for terms added by this bill, including "cross-cutting," "customer service measure," "efficiency measure," and "milestone."

Section 4. Performance Reporting Amendments

This section amends section 1116 of title 31, United States Code, which is retitled "Agency Performance Reporting."

This section requires the head of the agency to make agency per formance updates available on the agency's public website. It also requires the agency to provide a performance update at least annu ally, occurring no later than 150 days after the end of the fiscal year, with agencies encouraged to provide more frequent updates for performance indicators that provide significant value to the fed eral government, Congress, or other key stakeholders, at a reason able level of administrative burden. Among other things, these up dates are required to include a review of the agency's success in achieving its performance goals, along with results for the five pre ceding fiscal years; and information about the reliability and valid ity of the data used to measure the agency's progress towards its performance goals. Agencies are also required to provide perform ance updates for classified program activities in the classified ap pendix of the agency performance plan.

Finally, where an agency has not met its performance goals, this section requires that the head of the agency submit a performance improvement plan to OMB; where there have been unmet perform ance goals for two consecutive years, the agency head is required to submit additional information to

Congress and to describe addi tional funding the agency will obligate to achieve the relevant goals.

Section 5. Federal Government and Agency Priority Goals

This section amends title 31, United States Code, by adding a new subsection 1120, "Federal Government and Agency Priority Goals."

This section requires the Director of OMB to coordinate with agencies to develop federal government priority goals, with the aim of improving performance and management across the federal gov ernment.

This section also provides the process for developing the federal government priority goals and making them available to the public. At a minimum, the goals are required to be posted on the government-wide performance website provided under the new section 1122 of title 31, United States Code, created by section 7 of this bill. The bill provides flexibility for the Director of OMB to make adjustments to the goals during the fouryear timeframe should there be significant changes in the federal government's operating environment. When developing or adjusting the goals, and at least once per Congress, the Director of OMB is also required to consult with key congressional committees and obtain both majority and minority views on the draft goals.

Further, this section requires the head of each of the 24 CFO Act agencies (or those otherwise determined by the Director of OMB) to identify agency priority goals from among the agency's perform ance goals. This section provides the Director of OMB the authority to determine the total number of agency priority goals across the federal government, as well as the number of priority goals to be developed by each agency.

Section 6. Quarterly Priority Progress Reviews and Use of Performance Information

This section amends title 31, United States Code, by adding a new subsection 1121, "Quarterly Priority Progress Reviews and Use of Performance Information."

This section lays out a process for reviewing progress towards the federal government priority goals on a quarterly basis at min imum. The Director of OMB, with the support of the PIC, is re quired to review with the appropriate lead government official the progress achieved during the most recent quarter, overall trend data, and the likelihood of meeting the performance target, among other things.

Officials from relevant agencies, organizations and program activities are to be included in the review, and the reviews are to assess whether the agencies, organizations, program activi ties, regulations, tax expenditures, policies and other activities are contributing as planned to each federal government priority.

In addition, the Director of OMB, with the support of the PIC, is re quired to categorize the federal government priority goals by their risk of not meeting their performance targets, and for those at greatest risk, identify strategies to improve performance.

This section also requires that, at each agency, the head of the agency and the agency's COO, with the support of the agency PIO, conduct an analogous quarterly review to review priority goals with the appropriate goal leaders.

Section 7. Transparency of Federal Government Programs, Priority Goals, and Results

This section amends title 31, United States Code, by adding a new subsection 1122, "Transparency of Programs, Priority Goals, and Results."

This section requires OMB to develop a single government-wide performance website by October 1, 2012 and update the informa tion presented on the website at least quarterly.

The website is re quired to include information on each program identified by the agencies, including a description of the purposes of each program and how the program contributes to the mission and goals of the agency, as well as the level of funding for each program for the cur rent and previous two fiscal years.

This section also requires the head of each agency to develop agency priority goals and to provide information about those pri ority goals for the website, including a description of how the goal will be achieved; the performance indicators to be used in assessing progress; the accuracy and reliability of the data used to measure progress towards the goals; and the results achieved.

The Director of OMB is also to make information on federal government priority goals available on the website.

Section 8. Agency Chief Operating Officers

This section amends title 31, United States Code, by adding a new subsection 1123, "Chief Operating Officers," establishing in statute the position of COO at each agency.

This section designates the deputy head of agency, or equivalent, at each agency as the agency's COO, with overall responsibility for improving the management and performance of the agency. Addi tional responsibilities include advising and assisting the head of agency in carrying out the planning and reporting requirements of this bill; overseeing agencyspecific efforts to improve management within the agency and across the federal government; and coordi nating with relevant personnel within and external to the agency who have a significant role in contributing to the mission and goals of the agency.

Section 9. Agency Performance Improvement Officers and the PerFormance Improvement Council

This section amends title 31, United States Code, by adding a new subsection 1124, "Performance Improvement Officers and the Performance Improvement Council," which establishes in statute the position of Performance Improvement Officer at each agency and a Performance Improvement Council.

This section directs the head of each agency, in consultation with the agency COO, to designate a senior executive at the agency as the agency PIO and describes the functions of the PIO. These func tions include to advise or assist the agency head and COO in se lecting agency goals; overseeing the implementation of the agency strategic planning, performance planning, and reporting require ments; conducting regular reviews of agency performance; and de veloping and using performance measures in personnel perform ance appraisals within the agency. The PIO is also responsible for ensuring that agency progress toward the achievement of all goals is communicated to leaders, managers, and employees in the agen cy and Congress, and is made available on the agency's public website.

This section also establishes a Performance Improvement Council to be chaired by the OMB Deputy Director for Management and which is to include the PIO from each CFO Act agency, and other PIOs and individuals as determined appropriate by the chair person. This section further sets out the responsibilities of the PIC, including assisting the Director of OMB to improve the perform ance of the federal government and achieve federal government pri ority goals and implement the planning, reporting, and use of performance information requirements related to federal government priority goals. The PIC is also to work to resolve specific government-wide or cross-cutting performance issues; facilitate the ex change among agencies of practices that have led to performance improvements within specific programs, agencies or across agen cies; and develop recommendations to streamline and improve per formance management policies and requirements.

This section also directs the Administrator of General Services to provide administrative and other support for the PIC to implement this section.

Section 10. Format of Performance Plans and Reports

This section requires agencies to produce all strategic plans, per formance plans, and performance reports in searchable, machine readable formats beginning in fiscal year 2012. Additionally, this section prohibits agencies from incurring expenses to print such plans and reports for external release, except for when providing such documents to the Congress. Instead, such plans and reports are to be made available on the government-wide performance website established by this bill. This section further requires the Director of OMB to issue guidance to agencies, not later than June 1, 2012, to provide concise and timely performance information for publication on the website.

Section 11. Reducing Duplicative and Outdated Agency Reporting

This section amends title 31, United States Code, to provide a process to eliminate or consolidate duplicative and outdated agency plans and reports.

This section requires each agency's COO to compile a list of all plans and reports the agency produces for Congress, either by law or as directed in congressional reports, and to identify those plans and reports that are outdated or duplicative of other required plans and reports. Each agency's COO is then to provide this information to the Director of OMB. This section further requires that the President is to include in each budget of the United States Government the list of duplicative or outdated plans. In addition, the sec tion authorizes the Director of OMB to submit proposed legislation to Congress to eliminate or consolidate such plans and reports.

Finally, this section requires that during the first year of imple mentation of this section, each agency's list of outdated and dupli cative plans and reports must comprise at least 10 percent of all plans and reports identified. In subsequent years, the Director of OMB will determine the minimum percentage to be listed by agen cies as outdated or duplicative.

Section 12. Performance Management Skills and Competencies

This section requires the Director of OPM, in consultation with the PIC, to identify key skills and competencies related to perform ance management in the federal government not later than one year after the enactment date of this Act. Not later than two years after the enactment of this Act, the Director of OPM must incor porate such skills and competencies into relevant position classi fications and agency training.

Section 13. Technical and Conforming Amendments

This section provides for several technical and conforming amendments to title 5 and title 31, United States Code.

Section 14. Implementation of This Act

This section provides timeframes for implementing this Act, in cluding interim planning and reporting activities. The Director of OMB, in coordination with agencies, is required to develop interim federal government priority goals and performance plans consistent with the requirements of this Act beginning with the submission of the Fiscal Year 2013 Budget of the United States Government. Also by the time the fiscal year 2013 budget is required to be sub mitted (February 6, 2012), agencies are required to make adjust ments to their strategic plans to bring them in line with the re quirements of this Act. Agencies must also begin making perform ance reporting updates consistent with the requirements of this Act beginning in fiscal year 2012 and, for fiscal year 2013, submit per formance plans consistent with the requirements of this Act.

This section also provides that the quarterly priority progress re views required under section 6 of this Act. Agency reviews of their progress achieved toward priority goals will begin for agencies with the first full quarter beginning on or after the date of enacting of this Act for the priority goals contained in the Analytical Perspec tives volume of the Fiscal Year 2011 Budget of the United States Government. Reviews of progress achieved toward the federal gov ernment priority goals are required to begin with the quarter end ing June 20, 2012.

This section further requires the Director of OMB to prepare guidance for agencies regarding the implementation of this Act.

Section 15. Congressional Oversight and Legislation

This section provides that nothing in this Act is to be construed as limiting the ability of Congress to establish, amendment, sus pend, or annual a goal of the federal government or an agency and requires several GAO reviews. These include reviews of this Act's implementation over time.

V. Evaluation of Regulatory Impact

Pursuant to the requirements of paragraph 11(b) of rule XXVI of the Standing Rules of the Senate, the Committee has considered the regulatory impact of this bill. The Congressional Budget Office states that the bill contains no intergovernmental or privatesector mandates as defined in the Unfunded Mandate Reform Act and would not affect the budgets of state, local, or tribal governments. The enactment of this legislation will not have significant regu latory impact.

VI. Congressional Budget Office Cost Estimate

November 9, 2010.
Hon. Joseph I. Lieberman,
Chairman,
Committee on Homeland Security and Governmental Affairs,
U.S. Senate, Washington, DC.

Dear Mr. Chairman: The Congressional Budget Office has pre pared the enclosed cost estimate for H.R. 2142, the GPRA Mod ernization Act of 2010.

If you wish further details on this estimate, we will be pleased to provide them. The CBO staff contact is Matthew Pickford.

Sincerely,
Douglas W. Elmendorf.

Enclosure

H.R. 2142—GPRA Modernization Act of 2010

H.R. 2142 would amend the Government Performance and Re sults Act of 1993 (GPRA), which requires federal agencies to define their missions and evaluate their performance. Specifically, the leg islation would require federal agencies to expand their efforts to track and improve performance by: providing the Congress and the public with additional information on their current plans; incor porating their management goals and improvement plans into the GPRA performance evaluation process; and providing information on their performance via the Internet. In addition, the legislation would require training for employees who analyze and evaluate government programs, a report by the Government Accountability Office (GAO), and a study by the Office of Personnel Management regarding the evaluation of government programs.

Some provisions of H.R. 2142 would codify current policies and executive orders, including requirements that chief operating offi cers in each agency manage the performance and improvement process, appoint Performance Improvement Officers, and create and evaluate the Performance Improvement Council. Because those provisions of the bill are being carried out under current policies and executive orders, CBO estimates that implementing them would result in no additional federal costs.

GPRA requires all federal agencies to prepare performance plans annually and strategic plans every three years. Based on informa tion from GAO, the Office of Management and Budget (OMB), and the Department of the Treasury, CBO estimates that the federal government spends between $50 million and $100 million annually to comply with current GPRA requirements.

Under the bill, CBO expects that most agencies' administrative workload would increase to carry out some of the requirements. In particular, additional costs would accrue from expanding public re porting on agencies' plans and performance, incorporating manage ment goals and improvement plans into GPRA, and providing addi tional training for employees. We estimate that additional spending among the 23 major federal agencies would vary significantly but average around $1 million a year each to implement those new re quirements. In total, CBO estimates that implementing H.R. 2142 would expand GPRA requirements and increase spending $75 mil lion government-wide over the 2011–2015 period, assuming the availability of appropriated funds. The legislation would affect direct spending by agencies not fund ed through annual appropriations, such as the Bonneville Power Administration and the Federal Deposit Insurance Corporation; therefore, payasyougo procedures apply.

However, CBO estimates that any change in spending by those agencies would not be signifi cant. Enacting H.R. 2142 would not affect revenues. Finally, implementing H.R. 2142 eventually could lead to more effective management of government agencies at a reduced cost. Additionally, placing more reporting online could result in lower costs in the future. All such savings would be discretionary, would depend on amounts provided in future appropriation acts, and would be small over the next five years. H.R. 2142 contains no intergovernmental or privatesector man dates as defined in the Unfunded Mandates Reform Act and would not affect the budgets of state, local, or tribal governments.

On June 7, 2010, CBO transmitted a cost estimate for H.R. 2142, the Government Efficiency, Effectiveness, and Performance Act of 2010, as ordered reported by the House Committee on Oversight and Government Reform on May 20, 2010. Both versions of the leg islation would change the Government Performance and Results Act of 1993, but in different ways. CBO's cost estimates reflect those differences.

The CBO staff contact for this estimate is Matthew Pickford. This estimate was approved by Theresa Gullo, Deputy Assistant Director for Budget Analysis.

VII. Changes in Existing Law Made by the Bill, as Reported

In compliance with paragraph 12 of rule XXVI of the Standing Rules of the Senate, changes in existing law made by H.R. 2142, as reported, are shown as follows (existing law proposed to be omit ted is enclosed in brackets, new matter is printed in italic, and ex isting law in which no change is proposed is shown in roman):

TITLE 5—GOVERNMENT ORGANIZATION AND EMPLOYEES
PART 1—THE AGENCIES GENERALLY
CHAPTER 3—POWERS

Sec. 306. *Agency* Strategic Plans

(a) [No later than September 30, 1997] *Not later than the first Monday in February of any year following the year in which the term of a President commences under section 101 of title 3,* the head of each agency shall [submit to the Director of the Office of Man agement and Budget] *make available on the public website of the agency a strategic plan and notify the President* and [to the] Con gress *of its availability* [a strategic plan for program activities]. Such plan shall contain—

(1) a comprehensive mission statement covering the major functions and operations of the agency;

(2) general goals and objectives, including outcomeoriented goals, for the major functions and operations of the agency;

(3) a description of how any goals and objectives contribute to the federal government priority goals required by section 1120(a) of title 31;

([3]*4*) a description of how the goals and objectives are to be achieved, including—

(A) a description of the operational processes, skills and technology, and the human, capital, information, and other resources required to [meet] *achieve* those goals and objec tives; *and*

(B) a description of how the agency is working with other agencies to achieve its goals and objectives as well as rel evant federal government priority goals;

(5) a description of how the goals and objectives incorporate views and suggestions obtained through congressional consulta tions required under subsection (d);

([4]*6*) a description of how the performance goals [included] *provided* in the plan required by section 1115(a) of title 31 [shall be related], *including the agency priority goals required by section 1120(b) of title 31, if applicable, contribute* to the general goals and objectives in the strategic plan;

([5]*7*) an identification of those key factors external to the agency and beyond its control that could significantly affect the achievement of the general goals and objectives; and

([6]*8*) a description of the program evaluations used in es tablishing or revising general goals and objectives, with a schedule for future program evaluations *to be conducted.*

(b) The strategic plan shall cover a period of not less than [5] *4* years following the fiscal year in which the plan is submitted.

As needed, the head of the agency may make adjustments to the stra tegic plan to reflect significant changes in the environment in which the agency is operating, with appropriate notification of Congress.

[The strategic plan shall be updated and revised at least every three years, except that the strategic plan for the Department of Defense shall be updated and revised at least every four years.]

(c) The performance plan required by section 1115*(b)* of title 31 shall be consistent with the agency's strategic plan. A performance plan may not be submitted for a fiscal year not covered by a cur rent strategic plan under this section.

(d) When developing *or making adjustments to a strategic plan*, the agency shall consult *periodically* with the Congress, *including majority and minority views from the appropriate authorizing, ap propriations, and oversight committees,* and shall solicit and con sider the views and suggestions of those entities potentially af fected by or interested in such a plan.

The agency shall consult with the appropriate committees of Congress at least once every 2 years.

(e) The functions and activities of this section shall be considered to be inherently governmental functions. The drafting of strategic plans under this section shall be performed only by federal employ ees.

(f) For purposes of this section the term 'agency' means an Executive agency defined under section 105, but does not include the Central Intelligence Agency, the Government Accountability Office, [the Panama Canal Commission,] the United States Postal Serv ice, and the Postal Regulatory Commission.

TITLE 31—MONEY AND FINANCE
SUBTITLE II—THE BUDGET PROCESS
CHAPTER 11—THE BUDGET AND FISCAL, BUDGET, AND PROGRAM INFORMATION

Sec. 1105. Budget Contents and Submission to Congress

(a) On or after the first Monday in January but not later than the first Monday in February of each year, the President shall sub mit a budget of the United States Government for the following fis cal year. Each budget shall include a budget message and sum mary and supporting information. The President shall include in each budget the following:

* * *

(37) the list of plans and reports, as provided for under sec tion 1125, that agencies identified for elimination or consolida tion because the plans and reports are determined outdated or duplicative of other required plans and reports.

* * *

Sec. 1115. Federal Government and Agency Performance Plans

(a) *Federal Government Performance Plans.*—In carrying out the provisions of section 1105(a)(28), the Director of the Office of Management and Budget shall [require each agency to prepare an annual performance plan covering each program activity set forth in the budget of such agency. Such plan shall—] *coordinate with agencies to develop the federal government performance plan. In addition to the submission of such plan with the budget of the United States Government, the Director of the Office of Management and Budget shall ensure that all information required by this sub section is concurrently made available on the website provided under section 1122 and updated periodically, but not less than an nually. The federal government performance plan shall—*

(1) establish federal government performance goals to define the level of performance to be achieved during the year in which the plan is submitted and the next fiscal year for each of the federal government priority goals required under section 1120(a) of this title;

(2) identify the agencies, organizations, program activities, regulations, tax expenditures, policies, and other activities con tributing to each federal government performance goal during each fiscal year;

(3) for each federal government performance goal, identify a lead government official who shall be responsible for coordi nating the efforts to achieve the goal;

(4) establish common federal government performance indicators with quarterly targets to be used in measuring or assessing—

(A) overall progress toward each federal government per formance goal; and

(B) the individual contribution of each agency, organiza tion, program activity, regulation, tax expenditure, policy, and other activity identified under paragraph (2);

(5) establish clearly defined quarterly milestones; and

(6) identify major management challenges that are Government-wide or cross-cutting in nature and describe plans to address such challenges, including relevant performance goals, performance indicators, and milestones.

(b) Agency Performance Plans.—Not later than the first Mon day in February of each year, the head of each agency shall make available on a public website of the agency, and notify the President and the Congress of its availability, a performance plan covering each program activity set forth in the budget of such agency. Such plan shall—

(1) establish performance goals to define the level of perform ance to be achieved by a program activity *during the year in which the plan is submitted and the next fiscal year*;

(2) express such goals in an objective, quantifiable, and measurable form unless authorized to be in an alternative form under subsection ([b]*c*);

(3) describe how the performance goals contribute to—

(A) the general goals and objectives established in the agency's strategic plan required by section 306(a)(2) of title 5; and

(B) any of the federal government performance goals es tablished in the federal government performance plan required by subsection (a)(1);

(4) identify among the performance goals those which are designated as agency priority goals as required by section 1120(b) of this title, if applicable;

([3]*5*) provide a description of how the performance goals [and objectives] are to be achieved, including—

(A) the operation*al* processes, training, skills and tech nology, and the human, capital, information, and other re sources and strategies required to meet those performance goals [and objectives];

(B) clearly defined milestones;

(C) an identification of the organizations, program activities, regulations, policies, and other activities that contribute to each performance goal, both within and external to the agency;

(D) a description of how the agency is working with other agencies to achieve its performance goals as well as relevant federal government performance goals; and

(E) an identification of the agency officials responsible for the achievement of each performance goal, who shall be known as goal leaders;

([4]*6*) establish *a balanced set of* performance indicators to be used in measuring or assessing [the relevant outputs, serv ice levels, and outcomes of each program activity] *progress to ward each performance goal, including, as appropriate, cus tomer service, efficiency, output, and outcome indicators;*

([5]*7*) provide a basis for comparing actual program results with the established performance goals; [and]

([6]*8*) [describe] *a description of how the agency will ensure the accuracy and reliability of the data used to measure progress towards its performance goals, including an identifica tion of—values;*

(B) the sources for these data;

(C) the level of accuracy required for the intended use of the data;

(D) any limitations to these data at the required level of accuracy; and

(E) how the agency will compensate for such limitations if needed to reach the required level of accuracy;

(9) describe major management challenges the agency faces and identify—

(A) planned actions to address such challenges;

(B) performance goals, performance indicators, and milestones to measure progress toward resolving such challenges; and

(C) the agency official responsible for resolving such challenges; and

(10) identify lowpriority program activities based on an analysis of their contribution to the mission and goals of the agency and include an evidencebased justification for designating a program activity as lowpriority.

([b]*c*) *Alternative Form.*—If an agency, in consultation with the Director of the Office of Management and Budget, determines that it is not feasible to express the performance goals for a par ticular program activity in an objective, quantifiable, and measur able form, the Director of the Office of Management and Budget may authorize an alternative form. Such alternative form shall—

(1) include separate descriptive statements of— (A)(i) a minimally effective program; and

(ii) a successful program; or

(B) such alternative as authorized by the Director of the Office of Management and Budget, with sufficient preci sion and in such terms that would allow for an accurate, independent determination of whether the program activi ty's performance meets the criteria of the description; or

(2) state why it is infeasible or impractical to express a per formance goal in any form for the program activity.

([c]*d*) *Treatment Of Program Activities.*—For the purpose of complying with this section, an agency may aggregate, disag gregate, or consolidate program activities, except that any aggrega tion or consolidation may not omit or minimize the significance of any program activity constituting a major function or operation for the agency.

([d]*e*) *Appendix.*—An agency may submit with its annual per formance plan an appendix covering any portion of the plan that— (1) is specifically authorized under criteria established by an Executive order to be kept secret in the interest of national defense or foreign policy; and

(2) is properly classified pursuant to such Executive order. ([e]*f*) *Inherently Governmental Functions.*—The functions and activities of this section shall be considered to be inherently governmental functions. The drafting of performance plans under this section shall be performed only by federal employees.

([f]*g*) *Chief Human Capital Officers.*—With respect to each agency with a Chief Human Capital Officer, the Chief Human Cap plan described under subsection [(a)(3)]*(b)(5)(A).*

([g]*h*) *Definitions.*—For purposes of this section and sections 1116 through [1119] *1125*, and sections 9703 and 9704, the term— (1) 'agency' has the same meaning as such term is defined under section 306(f) of title 5;

(2) 'cross-cutting' means across organizational (such as agency) boundaries;

(3) 'customer service measure' means an assessment of service delivery to a customer, client, citizen, or other recipient, which can include an assessment of quality, timeliness, and satisfac tion among other factors;

(4) 'efficiency measure' means a ratio of a program activity's inputs (such as costs or hours worked by employees) to its out puts (amount of products or services delivered) or outcomes (the desired results of a program);

(5) 'major management challenge' means programs or management functions, within or across agencies, that have greater vulnerability to waste, fraud, abuse, and mismanagement (such as issues identified by the Government Accountability Office as high risk or issues identified by an Inspector General) where a failure to perform well could seriously affect the ability of an agency or the government to achieve its mission or goals;

(6) 'milestone' means a scheduled event signifying the completion of a major deliverable or a set of related deliverables or a phase of work;

([2]*7*) 'outcome measure' means an assessment of the results of a program activity compared to its intended purpose;

([3]*8*) 'output measure' means the tabulation, calculation, or recording of activity or effort and can be expressed in a quan titative or qualitative manner;

([4]*9*) 'performance goal' means a target level of perform ance expressed as a tangible, measurable objective, against which actual achievement can be compared, including a goal expressed as a quantitative standard, value, or rate;

([5]*10*) 'performance indicator' means a particular value or characteristic used to measure output or outcome;

([6]*11*) 'program activity' means a specific activity or project as listed in the program and financing schedules of the annual budget of the United States Government; and

([7]*12*) 'program evaluation' means an assessment, through objective measurement and systematic analysis, of the manner and extent to which federal programs achieve intended objec tives.

* * *

Sec. 1116. [Program] *Agency* Performance Report*ing*[S]

(a) [Not later than 150 days after the end of an agency's fiscal year, t]*T*he head of each agency shall [prepare and submit to the President and the Congress, a report on agency performance for the previous fiscal year] *make available on a public website of the agency an update on agency performance.*

(b)(1) Each [program performance report] *update* shall [set forth the performance indicators] *compare actual performance achieved with the performance goals* established in the agency performance plan under section

1115*(b)* [along with the actual performance achieved compared with the performance goals expressed in the plan for that fiscal year] *and shall occur no less than 150 days after the end of the fiscal year, with more frequent updates of actual performance on indicators that provide data of significant value to the government, Congress, or program partners at a reasonable level of administrative burden.*

(2) If performance goals are specified in an alternative form under section 1115([b]*c*), the results [of such a program] shall be described in relation to such specifications, including whether the performance failed to meet the criteria of a minimally effective or successful program.

[(c) The report for fiscal year 2000 shall include actual results for the preceding fiscal year, the report for fiscal year 2001 shall include actual results for the two preceding fiscal years, and the re port for fiscal year 2002 and all subsequent reports shall include actual results for the three preceding fiscal years.]

([d]*c*) Each [report] *update* shall—

(1) review the success of achieving the performance goals [of the fiscal year] *and include actual results for the five preceding fiscal years*;

(2) evaluate the performance plan for the current fiscal year relative to the performance achieved toward the performance goals [in the fiscal year covered by the report] *during the period covered by the update*;

(3) explain and describe where a performance goal has not been met (including when a program activity's performance is determined not to have met the criteria of a successful program activity under section 1115([b]*c*)(1)(A)(ii) or a corresponding level of achievement if another alternative form is used)—

(A) why the goal was not met;

(B) those plans and schedules for achieving the established performance goal; and

(C) if the performance goal is impractical or infeasible, why that is the case and what action is recommended;

(4) describe the use and assess the effectiveness in achieving performance goals of any waiver under section 9703 of this title;

(5) include a review of the performance goals and evaluation of the performance plan relative to the agency's strategic human capital management; [and]

(6) describe how the agency ensures the accuracy and reliability of the data used to measure progress towards its performance goals, including an identification of—

(A) the means to be used to verify and validate measured values;
(B) the sources for these data;
(C) the level of accuracy required for the intended use of the data;
(D) any limitations to these data at the required level of accuracy; and
(E) how the agency has compensated for such limitations if needed to reach the required level of accuracy; and

([6]7) include the summary findings of those program eval uations completed during the fiscal year covered by the report. *(d) If an agency performance update includes any program activity or information that is specifically authorized under criteria es tablished by an Executive Order to be kept secret in the interest of national defense or foreign policy and is properly classified pursu ant to such Executive Order, the head of the agency shall make such information available in the classified appendix provided under sec tion 1115(e).*

[(e)(1) Except as provided in paragraph (2), each agency perform ance report shall contain an assessment by the agency head of the completeness and reliability of the performance data included in the report. The assessment shall describe any material inadequa cies in the completeness and reliability of the performance data, and the actions the agency can take and is taking to resolve such inadequacies.

[(2) If an agency performance report is incorporated into a report submitted under section 3516, the requirements of section 3516(e) shall apply in lieu of paragraph (1).]

([f]*e*) The functions and activities of this section shall be consid ered to be inherently governmental functions. The drafting of agen cy performance [reports] *updates* under this section shall be per formed only by federal employees.

* * *

Sec. 1120. Federal Government and Agency Priority Goals

(a) Federal Government Priority Goals—.

(1) The Director of the Office of Management and Budget shall coordinate with agencies to develop priority goals to improve the performance and management of the federal government.

Such federal government priority goals shall include—

(A) outcomeoriented goals covering a limited number of cross-cutting policy areas; and

(B) goals for management improvements needed across the federal government, including

(i) financial management;

(ii) human capital management;

(iii) information technology management;

(iv) procurement and acquisition management; and

(v) real property management;

(2) The federal government priority goals shall be long-term in nature. At a minimum, the federal government priority goals shall be updated or revised every 4 years and made publicly available concurrently with the submission of the budget of the United States Government made in the first full fiscal year following any year in which the term of the President commences under section 101 of title 3. As needed, the Director of the Office of Management and Budget may make adjustments to the federal government priority goals to reflect significant changes in the environment in which the federal government is operating, with appropriate notification of Congress.

(3) When developing or making adjustments to federal government priority goals, the Director of the Office of Management and Budget shall consult periodically with the Congress, including obtaining majority and minority views from—

(A) the Committees on Appropriations of the Senate and the House of Representatives;

(B) the Committees on the Budget of the Senate and the House of Representatives;

(C) the Committee on Homeland Security and Governmental Affairs of the Senate;

(D) the Committee on Oversight and Government Reform of the House of Representatives;

(E) the Committee on Finance of the Senate;

(F) the Committee on Ways and Means of the House of Representatives; and

(G) any other committees as determined appropriate.

(4) The Director of the Office of Management and Budget shall consult with the appropriate committees of Congress at least once every 2 years.

(5) The Director of the Office of Management and Budget shall make information about the federal government priority goals available on the website described under section 1122 of this title.

(6) The federal government performance plan required under section 1115(a) of this title shall be consistent with the federal government priority goals

(b) Agency Priority Goals—.

(1) Every 2 years, the head of each agency listed in section 901(b) of this title, or as otherwise determined by the Director of the Office of Management and Budget, shall identify agency priority goals from among the performance goals of the agency.

The Director of the Office of Management and Budget shall determine the total number of agency priority goals across the government, and the number to be developed by each agency.

The agency priority goals shall—

(A) reflect the highest priorities of the agency, as determined by the head of the agency and informed by the federal government priority goals provided under subsection

(a) and the consultations with Congress and other interested parties required by section 306(d) of title 5;

(B) have ambitious targets that can be achieved within a 2year period;

(C) have a clearly identified agency official, known as a goal leader, who is responsible for the achievement of each agency priority goal;

(D) have interim quarterly targets for performance indicators if more frequent updates of actual performance provides data of significant value to the government, Congress, or program partners at a reasonable level of administrative burden; and

(E) have clearly defined quarterly milestones.

(2) If an agency priority goal includes any program activity or information that is specifically authorized under criteria established by an Executive order to be kept secret in the interest of national defense or foreign policy and is properly classified pursuant to such Executive order, the head of the agency shall make such information available in the classified appendix provided under section 1115(e).

(c) The functions and activities of this section shall be considered to be inherently governmental functions. The development of federal government and agency priority goals shall be performed only by federal employees.

* * *

Sec. 1121. Quarterly Priority Progress Reviews and Use of Performance Information

(a) Use Of Performance Information To Achieve Federal Government Priority Goals.—Not less than quarterly, the Direc tor of the Office of Management and Budget, with the support of the Performance Improvement Council, shall—

(1) for each federal government priority goal required by sec tion 1120(a) of this title, review with the appropriate lead gov ernment official the progress achieved during the most recent quarter, overall trend data, and the likelihood of meeting the planned level of performance;

(2) include in such reviews officials from the agencies, organi zations, and program activities that contribute to the accom plishment of each federal government priority goal;

(3) assess whether agencies, organizations, program activities, regulations, tax expenditures, policies, and other activities are contributing as planned to each federal government priority goal;

(4) categorize the federal government priority goals by risk of not achieving the planned level of performance; and

(5) for the federal government priority goals at greatest risk of not meeting the planned level of performance, identify prospects and strategies for performance improvement, including any needed changes to agencies, organizations, program activities, regulations, tax expenditures, policies or other activities.

(b) Agency Use Of Performance Information To Achieve

Agency Priority Goals.—Not less than quarterly, at each agency required to develop agency priority goals required by section 1120(b) of this title, the head of the agency and Chief Operating Officer, with the support of the agency Performance Improvement Officer, shall—

(1) for each agency priority goal, review with the appropriate goal leader the progress achieved during the most recent quarter, overall trend data, and the likelihood of meeting the planned level of performance;

(2) coordinate with relevant personnel within and outside the agency who contribute to the accomplishment of each agency priority goal;

(3) assess whether relevant organizations, program activities, regulations, policies, and other activities are contributing as planned to the agency priority goals;

(4) categorize agency priority goals by risk of not achieving the planned level of performance; and

(5) for agency priority goals at greatest risk of not meeting the planned level of performance, identify prospects and strategies for performance improvement, including any needed changes to agency program activities, regulations, policies, or other activities.

* * *

Sec. 1122. Transparency of Programs, Priority Goals, and ReSults

(a) Transparency Of Agency Programs.—

(1) In General.—Not later than October 1, 2012, the Office of Management and Budget shall—

(A) ensure the effective operation of a single website;

(B) at a minimum, update the website on a quarterly basis; and

(C) include on the website information about each program identified by the agencies.

(2) INFORMATION.—Information for each program described under paragraph (1) shall include—

(A) an identification of how the agency defines the term program', consistent with guidance provided by the Director of the Office of Management and Budget, including the program activities that are aggregated, disaggregated, or consolidated to be considered a program by the agency;

(B) a description of the purposes of the program and the contribution of the program to the mission and goals of the agency; and

(C) an identification of funding for the current fiscal year and previous 2 fiscal years.

(b) Transparency Of Agency Priority Goals And Results.—

The head of each agency required to develop agency priority goals shall make information about each agency priority goal available to the Office of Management and Budget for publication on the website, with the exception of any information covered by section 1120(b)(2) of this title. In addition to an identification of each agency priority goal, the website shall also consolidate information about each agency priority goal, including

(1) a description of how the agency incorporated any views and suggestions obtained through congressional consultations about the agency priority goal;

(2) an identification of key factors external to the agency and beyond its control that could significantly affect the achieve ment of the agency priority goal;

(3) a description of how each agency priority goal will be achieved, including—

(A) the strategies and resources required to meet the pri ority goal;

(B) clearly defined milestones;

(C) the organizations, program activities, regulations, policies, and other activities that contribute to each goal, both within and external to the agency;

(D) how the agency is working with other agencies to achieve the goal; and

(E) an identification of the agency official responsible for achieving the priority goal;

(4) the performance indicators to be used in measuring or as sessing progress;

(5) a description of how the agency ensures the accuracy and reliability of the data used to measure progress towards the priority goal, including an identification of—

(A) the means used to verify and validate measured values;

(B) the sources for the data;

(C) the level of accuracy required for the intended use of the data;

(D) any limitations to the data at the required level of accuracy; and

(E) how the agency has compensated for such limitations if needed to reach the required level of accuracy;

(6) the results achieved during the most recent quarter and overall trend data compared to the planned level of performance;

(7) an assessment of whether relevant organizations, program activities, regulations, policies, and other activities are contributing as planned;

(8) an identification of the agency priority goals at risk of not achieving the planned level of performance; and

(9) any prospects or strategies for performance improvement.

(c) Transparency Of Federal Government Priority Goals

And Results.—The Director of the Office of Management and Budget shall also make available on the website—

(1) a brief description of each of the federal government priority goals required by section 1120(a) of this title;

(2) a description of how the federal government priority goals incorporate views and suggestions obtained through congressional consultations;

(3) the federal government performance goals and performance indicators associated with each federal government priority goal as required by section 1115(a) of this title;

(4) an identification of the lead government official for each federal government performance goal;

(5) the results achieved during the most recent quarter and overall trend data compared to the planned level of performance;

(6) an identification of the agencies, organizations, program activities, regulations, tax expenditures, policies, and other activities that contribute to each federal government priority goal;

(7) an assessment of whether relevant agencies, organizations, program activities, regulations, tax expenditures, policies, and other activities are contributing as planned;

(8) an identification of the federal government priority goals at risk of not achieving the planned level of performance; and

(9) any prospects or strategies for performance improvement.

(d) Information On Website.—The information made available on the website under this section shall be readily accessible and easily found on the Internet by the public and members and committees of Congress. Such information shall also be presented in a searchable, machinereadable format. The Director of the Office of Management and Budget shall issue guidance to ensure that such information is provided in a way that presents a coherent picture of all federal programs, and the performance of the federal government as well as individual agencies.

* * *

Sec. 1123. Chief Operating Officers

(a) Establishment.—At each agency, the deputy head of agen cy, or equivalent, shall be the Chief Operating Officer of the agency.

(b) Function.—Each Chief Operating Officer shall be respon sible for improving the management and performance of the agency, and shall—

(1) provide overall organization management to improve agency performance and achieve the mission and goals of the agency through the use of strategic and performance planning, measurement, analysis, regular assessment of progress, and use of performance information to improve the results achieved;

(2) advise and assist the head of agency in carrying out the requirements of sections 1115 through 1122 of this title and sec tion 306 of title 5;

(3) oversee agencyspecific efforts to improve management functions within the agency and across government; and

(4) coordinate and collaborate with relevant personnel within and external to the agency who have a significant role in con tributing to and achieving the mission and goals of the agency, such as the Chief Financial Officer, Chief Human Capital Offi cer, Chief Acquisition Officer/Senior Procurement Executive, Chief Information Officer, and other line of business chiefs at the agency.

* * *

Sec. 1124. Performance Improvement Officers and the Performance Improvement Council

(a) Performance Improvement Officers.—

(1) Establishment.—At each agency, the head of the agency, in consultation with the agency Chief Operating Officer, shall designate a senior executive of the agency as the agency Performance Improvement Officer.

(2) Function.—Each Performance Improvement Officer shall report directly to the Chief Operating Officer. Subject to the direction of the Chief Operating Officer, each Performance Improvement Officer shall—

(A) advise and assist the head of the agency and the Chief Operating Officer to ensure that the mission and goals of the agency are achieved through strategic and performance planning, measurement, analysis, regular assessment of progress, and use of performance information to improve the results achieved;

(B) advise the head of the agency and the Chief Operating Officer on the selection of agency goals, including opportunities to collaborate with other agencies on common goals;

(C) assist the head of the agency and the Chief Operating Officer in overseeing the implementation of the agency strategic planning, performance planning, and reporting requirements provided under sections 1115 through 1122 of this title and sections 306 of title 5, including the contributions of the agency to the federal government priority goals;

(D) support the head of agency and the Chief Operating Officer in the conduct of regular reviews of agency performance, including at least quarterly reviews of progress achieved toward agency priority goals, if applicable;

(E) assist the head of the agency and the Chief Operating Officer in the development and use within the agency of performance measures in personnel performance apprais als, and, as appropriate, other agency personnel and plan ning processes and assessments; and

(F) ensure that agency progress toward the achievement of all goals is communicated to leaders, managers, and em ployees in the agency and Congress, and made available on a public website of the agency.

(b) Performance Improvement Council.—

(1) Establishment.—There is established a Performance Improvement Council, consisting of—

(A) the Deputy Director for Management of the Office of Management and Budget, who shall act as chairperson of the Council;

(B) the Performance Improvement Officer from each agency defined in section 901(b) of this title;

(C) other Performance Improvement Officers as determined appropriate by the chairperson; and

(D) other individuals as determined appropriate by the chairperson.

(2) Function.—The Performance Improvement Council shall—

(A) be convened by the chairperson or the designee of the chairperson, who shall preside at the meetings of the Performance Improvement Council, determine its agenda, direct its work, and establish and direct subgroups of the Performance Improvement Council, as appropriate, to deal with particular subject matters;

(B) assist the Director of the Office of Management and Budget to improve the performance of the federal government and achieve the federal government priority goals;

(C) assist the Director of the Office of Management and Budget in implementing the planning, reporting, and use of performance information requirements related to the federal government priority goals provided under sections 1115, 1120, 1121, and 1122 of this title;

(D) work to resolve specific Government-wide or cross cutting performance issues, as necessary;

(E) facilitate the exchange among agencies of practices that have led to performance improvements within specific programs, agencies, or across agencies;

(F) coordinate with other interagency management councils;

(G) seek advice and information as appropriate from non member agencies, particularly smaller agencies;

(H) consider the performance improvement experiences of corporations, nonprofit organizations, foreign, State, and local governments, government employees, public sector unions, and customers of government services;

(I) receive such assistance, information and advice from

agencies as the Council may request, which agencies shall provide to the extent permitted by law; and

(J) develop and submit to the Director of the Office of Management and Budget, or when appropriate to the President through the Director of the Office of Management and Budget, at times and in such formats as the chairperson may specify, recommendations to streamline and improve performance management policies and requirements.

(3) Support.—

(A) In General.—The Administrator of General Services shall provide administrative and other support for the Council to implement this section.

(B) Personnel.—The heads of agencies with Performance Improvement Officers serving on the Council shall, as appropriate and to the extent permitted by law, provide at the request of the chairperson of the Performance Improve ment Council up to 2 personnel authorizations to serve at the direction of the chairperson.

* * *

Sec. 1125. Elimination of Unnecessary Agency Reporting

(a) Agency Identification Of Unnecessary Reports.—Annu ally, based on guidance provided by the Director of the Office of Management and Budget, the Chief Operating Officer at each agen cy shall—

(1) compile a list that identifies all plans and reports the agency produces for Congress, in accordance with statutory re quirements or as directed in congressional reports;

(2) analyze the list compiled under paragraph (1), identify which plans and reports are outdated or duplicative of other re quired plans and reports, and refine the list to include only the plans and reports identified to be outdated or duplicative;

(3) consult with the congressional committees that receive the plans and reports identified under paragraph

(2) to determine whether those plans and reports are no longer useful to the committees and could be eliminated or con solidated with other plans and reports; and

(4) provide a total count of plans and reports compiled under paragraph (1) and the list of outdated and duplicative reports identified under paragraph (2) to the Director of the Office of Management and Budget.

(b) Plans And Reports.—

(1) First Year.—During the first year of implementation of this section, the list of plans and reports identified by each agency as outdated or duplicative shall be not less than 10 percent of all plans and reports identified under subsection (a)(1).

(2) Subsequent Years.—In each year following the first year described under paragraph (1), the Director of the Office of Management and Budget shall determine the minimum percent of plans and reports to be identified as outdated or duplicative on each list of plans and reports.

(c) Request For Elimination Of Unnecessary Reports.—In addition to including the list of plans and reports determined to be outdated or duplicative by each agency in the budget of the United States government, as provided by section 1105(a)(37), the Director of the Office of Management and Budget may concurrently submit to Congress legislation to eliminate or consolidate such plans and reports.

End Notes

[1] P.L. 103–62.

[2] At that time, the Committee was known as the Governmental Affairs Committee.

[3] U.S. Senate Committee on Governmental Affairs, *Government Performance and Results Act, 1993 (to S. 20), Together with Dissenting and Separate Views*, (103 S. Rpt. 103–58), p. 2.

[4] GPRA, 2(a)(1) and 2(b)(5).

[5] This includes the Chief Financial Officers Act of 1990 (P.L. 111–204), as amended by the Government Management Reform Act of 1994 (P.L. 103–356), and information technology re form legislation, including the Paperwork Reduction Act of 1995 (P.L. 104–13) and the Clinger Cohen Act of 1996 (P.L. 104–106).

[6] GAO, *ResultsOriented Government: GPRA Has Established a Solid Foundation for Achieving Greater Results*, GAO–04–38 (Washington, D.C.: March 10, 2004) p. 25.

[7] *Ibid.*, "Highlights."

[8] *Ibid.*, p. 7.

[9] *Ibid.*, p. 9.

[10] *Ibid.*, p. 15.

[11] The PIO position and the PIC currently exist in the federal government, having been estab lished by Executive Order 13450, *Improving Government Program Performance*, on

November 13, 2007, available at *http://georgewbushwhitehouse.archives.gov/news/releases/2007/11/20071139.html*, last accessed on November 24, 2010.

[12] Committee on Governmental Affairs, *Government Performance and Results Act, 1993, (to S. 20), Together with Dissenting and Separate Views,* (103 S. Rpt. 103–58), p. 15.

[13] U.S. Government Accountability Office, *Agencies' Strategic Plans Under GPRA: Key Ques tions to Facilitate Congressional Review,* GAO Report GGD–10–1–16 (Washington: GAO, 1997), p. 9.

[14] GAO, *ResultsOriented Government: GPRA Has Established a Solid Foundation for Achiev ing Greater Results,* GAO–04–38 (Washington, D.C.: March 10, 2004), p. 92.

[15] Committee on Governmental Affairs, *Government Performance and Results Act, 1993 (to S. 20), Together with Dissenting and Separate Views,* (103 S. Rpt. 103–58), p. 18.

[16] GAO, *ResultsOriented Government: GPRA Has Established a Solid Foundation for Achiev ing Greater Results,* GAO–04–38 (Washington, D.C.: March 10, 2004), p. 26.

[17] GAO, *The Results Act: An Evaluator's Guide to Assessing Agency Annual Performance Plans,* GAO/GGD–10.1.20 (Washington, D.C.: April 1998).

[18] GAO, *Agencies' Annual Performance Plans under the Results Act: An Assessment Guide to Facilitate Congressional Decisionmaking,* GAO/GGD/AIMD–10.1.18 (Washington, D.C.: February 1998).

[19] GAO, *ResultsOriented Government: GPRA Has Established a Solid Foundation for Achiev ing Greater Results,* GAO–04–38 (Washington, D.C.: March 10, 2004), p. 20.

[20] *Ibid.,* p. 111.

[21] Committee on Governmental Affairs, *Government Performance and Results Act, 1993 (to S. 20), Together with Dissenting and Separate Views,* (103 S. Rpt. 103–58), p. 27.

[22] GAO, *The Results Act: Assessment of the Government-wide Performance Plan for Fiscal Year 1999,* GAO/AIMD/GGD–98–159 (Washington, D.C.: September 8, 1998), p. 6.

[23] GAO, *ResultsOriented Government: GPRA Has Established a Solid Foundation for Achiev ing Greater Results,* GAO–04–38 (Washington, D.C.: March 10, 2004), p. 94.

[24] *Ibid.,* p. 105.

[25] This legislation limits these agencies to the 24 CFO Act agencies, or as otherwise deter mined by the Director of OMB.

[26] GAO, *Highlights of a GAO Roundtable on the Chief Operating Officer (COO) Concept: A Po tential Strategy to Address Federal Governance Challenges,* GAO–03–192SP (Washington, D.C.: October 4, 2002), p. 8.

[27] The White House, *Presidential Memorandum, Implementing Management Reform in the Ex ecutive Branch,* (Washington, D.C.: October 1, 1993), available at *http://govinfo.library.unt.edu/ npr/library/direct/memos/2552.html,* last accessed on November 24, 2010. The White House, *Presidential Memorandum, Implementing Government Reform,* (Washington, D.C.: July 11, 2001), available at *http://georgewbush whitehouse.archives.gov/news/releases/2001/07/200107115.html,* last accessed on November 24, 2010.

[28] These include officials such as the Chief Acquisition Officer, Chief Financial Officer, Chief Human Capital Officer, Chief Information Officer, and other line of business chiefs.

[29] The White House, *Executive Order 13450, Improving Government Program Performance,* (Washington, D.C.: November 13, 2007), available at *http://georgewbush–whitehouse.archives.gov/news/releases/2007/11/200711139.html,* last accessed on November 24, 2010.

[30] Examples include the Chief Acquisition Officers Council, the Chief Financial Officers Coun cil, the Chief Human Capital Officers Council, the Chief Information Officers Council, and the Federal Real Property Management Council.

[31] GAO, *Government Performance: Lessons Learned for the Next Administration on Using Per formance Information to Improve Results,* GAO–08–1026T (Washington, D.C.: July 24, 2008), "What GAO Found."

[32] GAO, *Government Performance: Lessons Learned for the Next Administration on Using Per formance Information to Improve Results,* GAO–08–1026T (Washington, D.C.: July 24, 2008), p. 16.

[33] GAO, *ResultsOriented Government: GPRA Has Established a Solid Foundation for Achiev ing Greater Results,* GAO–04–38 (Washington, D.C.: March 10, 2004), pp. 9–10.

[34] GAO, *Performance Budgeting: Past Initiatives Offer Insights for GPRA Implementation,* GAO/AIMD–97–46 (Washington, D.C.: March 27, 1997), p. 4.

[35] Committee on Governmental Affairs, *Government Performance and Results Act, 1993 (to S. 20), Together with Dissenting and Separate Views,* (103 S. Rpt. 103–58), p. 25.

[36] For technical and conforming reasons, the Committee extended existing inherently governmental GPRA standards to the new federal government and agency priority goals created by this bill in section 31 U.S.C. § 1120(c), as well as the new section 31 U.S.C. § 1116(e), which updates agency performance 'reports' to be referred to as agency performance 'updates,' in ac cordance with H.R. 2142.

INDEX

A

B

C

D

E

F

G

H

I

J

L

M

N

O

P

Q

R

S